Exploring Tokyo
The Economic and Cultural Center of Japan

Coen Nishiumi

English editing by Ed Jacob

Special Edition

JN094936

IBC パブリッシング

Planning/Editing by iTEP Japan
All photographs by wikipedia, photoAC and photolibrary
Cover photo by photolibrary

はじめに

　ラダーシリーズは、「はしご（ladder）」を使って一歩一歩上を目指すように、学習者の実力に合わせ、無理なくステップアップできるよう開発された英文リーダーのシリーズです。

　リーディング力をつけるためには、繰り返したくさん読むこと、いわゆる「多読」がもっとも効果的な学習法であると言われています。多読では、「1.速く 2.訳さず英語のまま 3.なるべく辞書を使わず」に読むことが大切です。スピードを計るなど、速く読むよう心がけましょう（たとえば TOEIC® テストの音声スピードはおよそ1分間に150語です）。そして1語ずつ訳すのではなく、英語を英語のまま理解するくせをつけるようにします。こうして読み続けるうちに語感がついてきて、だんだんと英語が理解できるようになるのです。まずは、ラダーシリーズの中からあなたのレベルに合った本を選び、少しずつ英文に慣れ親しんでください。たくさんの本を手にとるうちに、英文書がすらすら読めるようになってくるはずです。

《本シリーズの特徴》

- 中学校レベルから中級者レベルまで5段階に分かれています。自分に合ったレベルからスタートしてください。
- クラシックから現代文学、ノンフィクション、ビジネスと幅広いジャンルを扱っています。あなたの興味に合わせてタイトルを選べます。
- 巻末のワードリストで、いつでもどこでも単語の意味を確認できます。レベル1、2では、文中の全ての単語が、レベル3以上は中学校レベル外の単語が掲載されています。
- カバーにヘッドホーンマークのついているタイトルは、オーディオ・サポートがあります。ウェブから購入／ダウンロードし、リスニング教材としても併用できます。

《使用語彙について》

レベル1：中学校で学習する単語約1000語

レベル2：レベル1の単語 ＋ 使用頻度の高い単語約300語

レベル3：レベル1の単語 ＋ 使用頻度の高い単語約600語

レベル4：レベル1の単語 ＋ 使用頻度の高い単語約1000語

レベル5：語彙制限なし

スペシャル・エディション：レベル3～4に相応。ただし、中学英語レベルでも無理なく読めるよう巻末のワードリストには全単語の意味を掲載しています。

Table of Contents

Chapter 7 Tokyo, the Priceless Inheritance of Edo Castle 111

読み始める前に

東京は言わずと知れた日本の首都で、日本経済の中心、そして文化の発信地でもあります。歴史や交通、見どころ満載の本書を読んで、英語でその魅力を感じてみましょう。

東京都の都章

東京都基本情報

都庁所在地：新宿区

面積：2,194.07km²（47都道府県中45番目・2020年）

人口：約1,400万人（47都道府県中1番目・2020年）

東京都の花：ソメイヨシノ *Somei-Yoshino*

東京都の木：イチョウ *Ginkgo*

東京都の鳥：ユリカモメ *Black-headed Gull*

気候と地形：東京都は、関東平野の南西に位置する内陸部と、東京湾から南方洋上に分布する島嶼部から成り立っています。内陸部は東西約85km、南北約25kmと細長く、東京23区（区部）と多摩地域に大別されます。区部の東は、隅田川、荒川、江戸川などの河口部に沖積平野が広がり、南の多摩川沿いは低地です。多摩川の北側は武蔵野台地、南側は多摩丘陵で、都の西部は関東山地の一部にあたります。島嶼部は火山活動によって形成された伊豆諸島と小笠原諸島があり、南北約1,200kmにわたります。

　気候は四季の変化が明瞭で、夏季は高温多湿に、冬季は晴れて空気が乾燥します。

　冬場の多摩地域は区部より気温が下がり、大雪になることもあります。伊豆諸島は一年を通して寒暖の差が小さく、小笠原諸島には梅雨がありません。

姉妹友好都市：アメリカ・ニューヨーク市、中国・北京、フランス・パリ、オーストラリア・ニューサウスウェールズ州、韓国・ソウル特別市、インドネシア・ジャカルタ特別市、ブラジル・サンパウロ州、エジプト・カイロ県、ロシア・モスクワ、ドイツ・ベルリン、イタリア・ローマ、イギリス・ロンドンの12都市と、都市行政・芸術・スポーツ・科学技術などの幅広い交流を行っています。

Chapter 1
Tokyo,
an Overview

Skyscrapers and Mt. Fuji (top),
Sumida-gawa River (bottom)

【東京都の概要】

東京都は日本全国で3番目に小さい都道府県ですが、日本の人口の10%以上が暮らしており、周辺地域を含めて世界最大の都市圏を形成しています。その経済規模はニューヨーク都市圏よりも大きく、日本、そして世界経済の中心都市です。東京から首都圏へ複雑に広がる鉄道網は、日々通勤・通学する無数の人々を運び、主要駅の1日の乗降客数は世界に類を見ない多さとなっています。

● わからない語は巻末のワードリストで確認しましょう。

- □ adjacent
- □ suburb
- □ humidity
- □ leisure
- □ complicated
- □ hub
- □ metropolis
- □ skyscraper

● 主な地名および名称、固有名詞

□ Greater Tokyo Area	大東京圏，首都圏
□ Kanto Plain	関東平野
□ Tokyo Bay	東京湾
□ Tama Region	多摩地域
□ Chiba Prefecture	千葉県
□ Saitama Prefecture	埼玉県
□ Yamanashi Prefecture	山梨県
□ Kanagawa Prefecture	神奈川県
□ Izu Islands	伊豆諸島
□ Bonin Islands	ボニン諸島
□ Ogasawara Islands	小笠原諸島
□ Sumida-gawa River	隅田川
□ Tama-gawa River	多摩川
□ Edo-gawa River	江戸川
□ Ara-kawa River	荒川
□ Kanda-gawa River	神田川
□ Imperial Palace	皇居
□ Edo Castle	江戸城

Population and economy

What comes to mind when you think of Tokyo?

A global economic and cultural center, the world's largest city, or a high-tech wonderland? It's all of these, and more. Let's take a closer look. There are over nine million people in the city's twenty-three wards (each of which is governed as a separate city within Tokyo), and if we count the adjacent cities as well, the Greater Tokyo Area has a combined population of over thirty-five million.

Without question, Tokyo is the economic and cultural center of Japan. As you may know, Japan is the world's third-largest economy. And the Greater Tokyo Area's GDP is the sixteenth largest in the world, right behind the nation of Russia. No other city has an economy as big as Tokyo's. It produced $US 1.6 trillion worth of goods and services in 2016, ahead of the number two city, New York, which generated $US 1.7 trillion.

Now you see why Tokyo is sometimes called a "monster city."

Geography

Tokyo is much more than just tall buildings and crowded streets. There are also mountains,

Tama Region
(Cities, Towns, Villages)

OKUTAMA-cho

OME City

MIZUHO-cho

KIYOSE City

HINODE-cho

HAMURA City

MUSASHI MURAYAMA City

HIGASHI YAMATO City

HIGASHI MURAYAMA City

HIGASHI KURUME City

HINOHARA-mura

AKIRUNO City

FUSSA City

TACHIKAWA City

KODAIRA City

NISHITOKYO City

AKISHIMA City

KOKUBUNJI City

KOGANEI City

MUSASHINO City

KUNITACHI City

MITAKA City

HACHIOJI City

HINO City

FUCHU City

CHOFU City

TAMA City

INAGI City

KOMAE City

MACHIDA City

Kanagawa Prefecture

forests, and even tropical islands. It is located in a large, flat area known as the Kanto Plain on the south coast of Honshu, Japan's main island.

The heart of the city are the twenty-three wards, which look a little like a fan spreading out from the east side of Tokyo Bay. These are home to the city's most famous areas, including Ginza, Akihabara, and Shinjuku. However, if

TOKYO

TOKYO 23 Wards

Saitama Prefecture

Chiba Prefecture

ITABASHI Ward
ADACHI Ward
KITA Ward
NERIMA Ward
KATSUSHIKA Ward
TOSHIMA Ward
ARAKAWA Ward
NAKANO Ward
BUNKYO Ward
TAITO Ward
SUMIDA Ward
SHINJUKU Ward
SUGINAMI Ward
CHIYODA Ward
EDOGAWA Ward
SHIBUYA Ward
KOTO Ward
CHUO Ward
MINATO Ward
SETAGAYA Ward
MEGURO Ward
SHINAGAWA Ward
OTA Ward

you continue heading west, there are twenty-six cities, five towns, and eight villages on the east side that are known as the Tama Region. These suburbs are where many of the city's workers live, enjoying larger homes and fresh air along the rail lines that lead into Tokyo.

The city is bordered by Chiba Prefecture to the east, Saitama Prefecture to the north, Yamanashi Prefecture to the west, and Kanagawa Prefecture to the south.

In addition to the twenty-three wards and the Tama Region, there are two island chains that are also officially part of Tokyo. The Izu Islands are often known as the "Seven Islands of Izu," although there are actually more than a dozen of them. Farther south are the Bonin Islands, which are more commonly known as the Ogasawara Islands. Both groups of islands are a popular vacation spot for Tokyo residents who want to enjoy sunshine, beaches, and swimming, surfing, or scuba-diving.

Tokyo's two largest rivers are the Sumida-gawa River, which flows from north to south into Tokyo Bay, and the Tama-gawa River, which flows from west to east. Other important waterways are the Edo-gawa, Ara-kawa, and Kanda-gawa Rivers.

Climate

Most people say the best time to visit Tokyo is in the late spring or early summer from April to early June, or in the autumn between September and late November, but there is really no season that is not a good time to visit.

Tokyo's winters are mild, and snow is rare, especially in the twenty-three wards. The cold season lasts from late November until early March, but the weather is generally sunny.

As temperatures begin to rise in March, Tokyo's cherry blossoms begin to bloom, usually around the end of the month. After that, the people of Tokyo enjoy some of the city's best weather in April, May, and early June, with sunny skies and warm temperatures.

The city's rainy season usually lasts from mid-June to late July, and although there can be many rainy days, sightseeing can still be enjoyable if

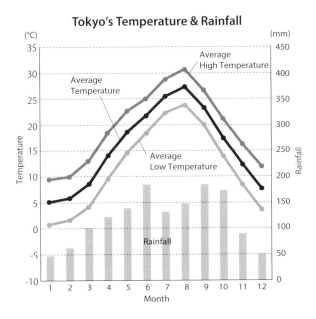

you plan your visits to indoor attractions for the wet-weather days.

Summer follows from late July to early September. While the temperatures and humidity levels do get high, nearly all businesses and residences are air-conditioned.

Fall is the time to see Tokyo's incredible autumn colors, and the leaves are usually most beautiful in mid-November. If you arrive earlier, though, it is possible to see them in the mountains on the west side of the city.

Transportation

Tokyo's incredible public transportation system is essential to its economic, social, and leisure activities.

There are 84 train lines and more than 1,500 stations in the Greater Tokyo Area. During the morning and evening rush hours, the huge population moves back and forth between the city's business centers and people's homes using the complicated network of commuter trains that links almost every area of the city like a giant spiderweb.

Oshiya

Once there were station employees called *oshiya*, or passenger pushers, at the major stations, and it was their job to push people into the crowded train cars. Although we barely see such chaos these days, countless passengers arrive at the major transportation hubs each day on their way to and from work.

The center of Tokyo?

If you ask where the center of Tokyo is, you may be told that it's the Imperial Palace, which is built on the site of Edo Castle. It is located literary in the center of Tokyo, very near Tokyo Station. However, there are more than ten business centers in this metropolis. And each business center is a hub for commuter trains and subways.

At night such business centers change their look. They shine brightly with the illumination and neon signs of the restaurants and *izakaya*, or traditional Japanese pubs, located in the valleys created by the city's skyscrapers.

Even though Tokyo is a relatively young city with a short history compared with Kyoto and Osaka, it has already become Japan's cultural hub.

Now let's start exploring the rich history of this metropolis.

Chapter 2
Tokyo's Rich History

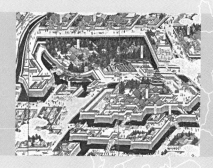

Perry's "Black Ships" (top),
Seventeenth-century painting of Edo Castle (bottom)

【東京の歴史】

かつて武蔵国の一角は、中世に割拠した江戸氏を由来とし、江戸と呼ばれました。室町時代に太田道灌が江戸城を築き、戦国時代を経て、徳川家康が幕府を開き、江戸は行政の中心地となります。1868年に江戸幕府が崩壊すると、江戸は東京と改称され、明治天皇が旧江戸城の皇居に移り、東京は近代日本の事実上の首都となりました。関東大震災や東京大空襲に遭いながら、その後の高度経済成長から現在に至るまで、日本の政治・経済の中心として発展を遂げています。

● わからない語は巻末のワードリストで確認しましょう。

- ☐ medieval
- ☐ strife
- ☐ feudal domain
- ☐ consolidate
- ☐ landfill
- ☐ canal
- ☐ administrative
- ☐ reconstruction

● 主な地名および名称、固有名詞

☐ Senso-ji (Temple)	浅草寺
☐ Edo clan	江戸氏
☐ Ota Dokan	太田道灌
☐ Oda Nobunaga	織田信長
☐ Toyotomi Hideyoshi	豊臣秀吉
☐ Tokugawa Ieyasu	徳川家康
☐ Venice	ヴェネチア，ヴェニス
☐ Tokugawa Iemitsu	徳川家光
☐ Van Gogh	ファン・ゴッホ
☐ Gauguin	ゴーガン（ポール・ゴーギャン）
☐ Commodore Perry	ペリー提督
☐ Emperor Meiji	明治天皇
☐ Great Kanto Earthquake	関東大震災
☐ World War Two	第二次世界大戦
☐ GHQ	連合国最高司令官総司令部
☐ Korean War	朝鮮戦争
☐ Michelin Guide	ミシュラン・ガイド

Beginnings

Of course, Tokyo did not develop overnight. Its history can be traced back over 1,400 years to the building of the city's first Buddhist temple, Senso-ji, in AD 645.

The area, which used to be called Edo, was nothing more than a tiny village until the end of the sixteenth century. Until that time, Japan's political and cultural center was in the area around Kyoto.

The name Edo comes from the Edo clan, which built a castle there in the eleventh century. After the clan's fall, the powerful warrior Ota Dokan took over the region in the fifteenth century. Historians believe that he converted Edo into a medieval town during a chaotic period when Japan was in a state of civil war.

Ota Dokan (1432–1486)

15

The unification of Japan

Tokugawa Ieyasu
(1543–1616)

Japan's history of internal strife and civil war during the fifteenth and sixteenth centuries is too long to summarize here, but the resulting weakness of many of the feudal domains led to the rise of three great figures. They are credited with reunifying Japan—Oda Nobunaga (1534–1582), Toyotomi Hideyoshi (1536–1598), and Tokugawa Ieyasu (1543–1616).

It was the last of these, Tokugawa, who moved to Edo and created his military headquarters there at the end of the sixteenth century. Then Tokugawa successfully united Japan and consolidated power under a military-dominated government after he was appointed shogun, or military dictator, by the emperor in Kyoto. He decided to move the administrative capital of Japan to Edo in 1603.

Although the city was much smaller back then, it has served as Japan's actual capital right up until the present day.

Building the city

After Tokugawa moved the *bakufu*, or shogunate government, to Edo at the beginning of the seventeenth century, a series of large-scale landfills was begun, and canals and moats were dug.

Many areas of swampy land, coves, and shallow areas of the bay were filled and became part of the city.

The construction of water supply systems allowed the people of Edo to access pure water in every neighborhood.

Tokyo, like Venice, became a city of rivers and canals that were traversed by boats. In the center of the city was Edo Castle, from which the Tokugawa-clan governed Japan.

Edo's social organization

At the same time they were shaping the city, the Tokugawa also shaped the society. A rigid social structure was put in place to control the *daimyo*, or feudal lords, so that the Tokugawa government would be able to remain in power. All the feudal lords were required to live in Edo for a certain period, so there were many large estates that enriched Edo's appearance.

Then to protect the safety of their capital, the Tokugawa created a police and firefighting system for the whole metropolitan area.

Alongside Edo Castle were areas like Akasaka and Kojimachi, which were where the highest-ranking warriors and feudal lords lived. Toward the current Tokyo Bay area, huge numbers of merchants and townspeople spent their days busily making and selling products. Even though the townspeople were low on the social ladder, they were Edo's cultural leaders.

The developing city

Known as the seat of administrative power during the Edo period, the city became a stronghold for the Tokugawa.

With a population of a million residents in the eighteenth century, Edo prospered as perhaps the world's largest and most densely populated city.

Not only did the samurai elite in the middle of the city make it a center of power, but it also bustled with the economic activities of the great numbers of merchants and craftsmen who helped sustain the elites' lifestyles and the vibrant economy as a whole.

In the era of the third shogun, Tokugawa Iemitsu, the government decided to close Japan's doors to foreigners, and the country remained shut off from the rest of the world until 1854.

Due to this policy, the people of Edo developed their own unique culture and lifestyle without influences from other countries.

Edo culture

Kabuki and other forms of theater, as well as arts such as ukiyo-e, or woodblock printing, originated and became popular during the Edo period. These genres catered to the masses but some of them, such as ukiyo-e, in particular, were exported to Europe after the Edo period.

Hiroshige "Sudden Shower Over Ohashi Bridge and Atake" (left),
Vincent van Gogh "Bridge in the Rain, after Hiroshige" (right)

Ukiyo-e is famous for influencing impressionists such as Van Gogh and Gauguin.

As for the food culture, sushi and many other famous Japanese delicacies were created by Edo's cooks.

Edo's customs and culture influenced not just the development of modern-day Tokyo, but the whole society of modern Japan, and some aspects have even spread internationally.

Disasters

Unfortunately, since Japanese houses were made of wood, Edo suffered from frequent fires.

Great fire of Meireki (1657)

Earthquakes also hit the city too. Due to such disasters, Edo was destroyed several times and had to be built again even though there were no wars or battles during the 250 years of Tokugawa rule. Even though very few of the houses built during the Edo period exist today, you will find the shadows and flavors of Edo in the old temples and alleys.

The end of Tokugawa rule

The peace of the Tokugawa shogunate was broken when Commodore Perry and his warships appeared off the shores near Edo and demanded that Japan its doors to the rest of the world in 1853.

Eventually, due to countless political problems, the Tokugawa's power declined.

Right after Perry's visit, Japan opened up to the outside world. Yokohama, located west of Edo, was chosen as a port where foreigners

Commodore Perry
(1794–1858)

Commodore Perry's visit to Kanagawa

could stay and trade. Because of this arrangement, eventually, Yokohama became a huge metropolis, and currently over two million people are living there, many of whom commute to Tokyo for work or school.

In 1868, Tokugawa rule finally ended. Edo was renamed Tokyo under the new government led by the emperor, whose followers had overthrown the Tokugawa to start a modern, centralized nation.

Up to that time, even though Edo was the administrative capital, the emperor's court was still located in Kyoto. After 1868, however,

Taisei Hokan (the Return of Political Power to the Emperor)

the emperor and his new government moved to Tokyo. Tokyo, in Japanese, means eastern capital as it is located far to the east of Kyoto. Since then, Tokyo has been serving as the nation's official capital.

Modernization

After the Tokugawa era ended, Western civilization began influencing Japan. In Ginza, the commercial center of Tokyo, many brick buildings were built, and gas lamps became a symbol of modernization. The first steam locomotive carried passengers between Tokyo and Yokohama in 1872.

In the era of Emperor Meiji, Japan gradually rose to power as a modern nation, and the lifestyles of Tokyo's citizens changed rapidly. After Japan won a war against Russia in 1905, Japan became known as a new power in the world, and Tokyo became the center of Japan's imperial system.

Hard times

Tokyo experienced some terrible events during the early and mid-twentieth century.

Tokyo had to be rebuilt twice after being hit by the Great Kanto Earthquake in 1923 and then being largely destroyed during World War Two. At this time, Tokyo was bombed

After bombing of Tokyo in March 1945

to ashes, and almost all buildings from the old city were wiped out.

Reconstruction

Tokyo's reconstruction started on August 15, 1945, when Japan surrendered to the allied nations at the end of World War Two. Japan was occupied by the US-led military, and it controlled the country from GHQ, or General Headquarters, in Tokyo.

Tokyo recovered from the war during the 1950s due to economic demand created by the Korean War. This led to Tokyo miraculously upgrading its infrastructure and economy in the 1960s.

Today, it is not only the seat of the government of Japan but a major economic center as well, with over fifty of the world's Fortune 500 companies, more than any other city in the world. Tokyo has been also ranked as the safest and most livable city on this planet, although it does suffer from natural disasters, such as earthquakes and typhoons.

A cosmopolitan city

As a measure of how cosmopolitan it has become, Tokyo has more restaurants with Michelin Guide stars than any other city in the world.

Once you enter this metropolis, you will enjoy its rich history, its economic dynamism, its cultural legacies, its fabulous cuisine, and its fascinating trends in fashion and innovation.

Chapter 3
Tokyo Survival Tactics

Suica (top),
Narita International Airport (bottom)

【東京を訪れるなら】

東京は世界でも有数の物価の高い都市です。また、無数の曲がりくねった道や路地を縫うように、さまざまな公共交通機関が運行しています。東京はお金がないと楽しめない？　地図や路線が入り組んでいて、動き回るのが難しい？　いいえ、そんなことはありません。東京でもお手頃な値段で、快適な衣食住を求めることができるのです。本章を読んで、東京を訪れる作戦を立てましょう。

● わからない語は巻末のワードリストで確認しましょう。

□ tactics	□ reasonable	□ accommodation
□ countless	□ transportation	□ crisscross
□ destination	□ seamless	

● 主な地名および名称、固有名詞

□ London	ロンドン
□ Paris	パリ
□ East Japan Railway (JR East)	東日本旅客鉄道（JR東日本）
□ Yamanote Line	山手線
□ Chuo and Sobu Lines	中央・総武線
□ Omiya	大宮
□ Suica	スイカ
□ PASMO	パスモ
□ Narita (International Airport)	成田国際空港
□ Narita Express	成田エクスプレス
□ Keisei Skyliner	（京成）スカイライナー
□ Haneda (Airport)	羽田空港
□ Keikyu Airport Line	京急空港線
□ Shinagawa Station	品川駅
□ Hakodate	函館
□ Kyushu	九州
□ Tokaido Shinkansen	東海道新幹線

Places to stay

There is a stereotypical image that Tokyo is an expensive place to visit or live in. It is true that if you want luxury, Tokyo is one of the most expensive places in the world. However, there are many tactics that will help you to enjoy Tokyo for a reasonable price.

For example, instead of choosing expensive international hotels with spacious rooms, you can look for so-called business hotels in Tokyo. Their rooms can be very small, but they provide everything you need. Most hotel rooms provide all the essential amenities, such as cotton robes, slippers, toothbrushes, toothpaste, and shaving kits.

If you are an adventurous traveler who wants to experience the real Japanese lifestyle, try a capsule hotel, which is sort of like a hotel dormitory. In these hotels, however, you can have privacy in a small capsule about 1.2 meters wide, 2 meters long, and 1 meter high, with your own TV and a nice, clean bed.

Speaking of hotels, there are also romantic accommodations called love hotels, which are for couples only. You can stay for the whole night or just for a few hours at any time of the day.

Eating cheaply

If you want to save money after trying a fancy meal at a traditional sushi restaurant, try the convenience stores that can be found all over the city. Convenience stores, known as *konbini*, sell almost all the snacks and useful items that you might need in daily life. You can get delicious ready-to-eat meals called *bento*, as well as inexpensive hot coffee at convenience stores. Additionally, most convenience stores have ATMs, photocopy machines, and tickets for major concerts, shows, and sporting events. If you need to go to the toilet, you can use one free of charge.

In addition to convenience stores, there are thousands of vending machines on the streets of Tokyo. They have countless varieties of drinks, although it is rare to find food in them.

Vending machines

Navigating

To survive in Tokyo, it's important to have some knowledge of the public transportation system.

First of all, you should know that it is very hard to get around Tokyo without a map or smartphone. Tokyo can be a difficult city to navigate, even for locals. Just like other cities with long histories, such as London or Paris, Tokyo has countless webs of winding streets and alleys.

Unfortunately, most of Tokyo's narrow streets don't have names. Instead, Tokyo addresses are determined by block numbers. Therefore, the GPS app on your tablet or smartphone will be very useful for getting around.

■ Trains and subways

The city of Tokyo is crisscrossed with train lines both above and below ground. It is the most extensive transportation network of any city in the world. Everything runs on time, and the subway cars are clean and quiet. However, as has already been mentioned, Tokyo trains are often very crowded during rush hour. You may find yourself standing *very* close to other people.

East Japan Railway, known as JR East, or sometimes just JR, operates the Yamanote Line, a loop line that goes around the center of the city. The Chuo and Sobu Lines cross the city from east to west. In addition, various other lines run from north to south, connecting Tokyo with Yokohama and points farther south, as well as Omiya and other destinations to the north.

If you want to move around the center of Tokyo, the Yamanote Line is very convenient because each station on the loop is also a hub that connects with subways and commuter lines.

In addition to the JR lines, there are privately owned railways branching out to the suburbs from several major JR stops, and over a dozen subway lines, also connecting the center of Tokyo to destinations throughout the metropolitan area.

The subway system might seem confusing at first, but it is color-coded and each station has a number. Signs and displays on the trains and in stations include English, as well as Chinese and Korean. If you're confused, English maps are also available at the stations at ticket gates and other areas.

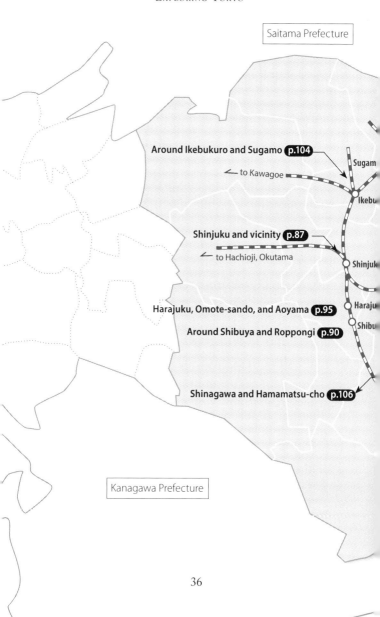

Saitama Prefecture

Around Ikebukuro and Sugamo p.104

Sugam

← to Kawagoe

Ikebu

Shinjuku and vicinity p.87

← to Hachioji, Okutama

Shinjuk

Harajuku, Omote-sando, and Aoyama p.95

Haraju

Around Shibuya and Roppongi p.90

Shibu

Shinagawa and Hamamatsu-cho p.106

Kanagawa Prefecture

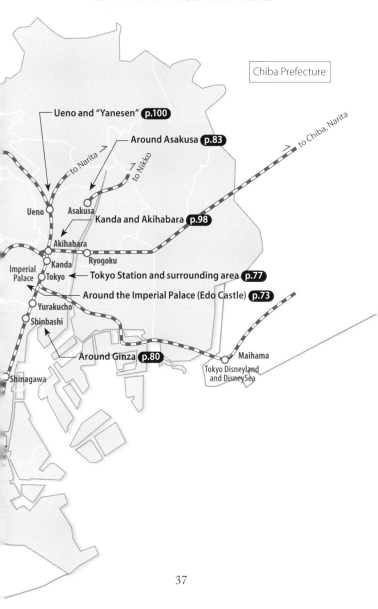

Chiba Prefecture

Ueno and "Yanesen" p.100

Around Asakusa p.83

to Chiba, Narita

to Narita

to Nikko

Ueno

Asakusa

Kanda and Akihabara p.98

Akihabara

Ryogoku

Imperial
Palace

Kanda

Tokyo   Tokyo Station and surrounding area p.77

Around the Imperial Palace (Edo Castle) p.73

Yurakucho

Shinbashi

Maihama

Tokyo Disneyland
and DisneySea

Around Ginza p.80

Shinagawa

37

■ Stations

Train stations in Tokyo can have many exits.
There are maps in the train station to show you
which exits are convenient for where you want
to go. Because some train stations are so big, it
is a good idea to make sure to choose the correct
exit, or you might have to walk a long way to
your destination.

Train tickets are purchased from vending
machines. If you buy a ticket for the wrong fare,
you can use the fare-adjustment machine just
inside the exit gates. You need your train ticket
or pass to exit the train station.

If you want to stay in Tokyo for more than a
day, it may be a good idea to purchase a *Suica* or
PASMO, which are rechargeable prepaid cards
that can also be used as electronic money. Both
Suica and PASMO are widely used throughout
Tokyo for transportation and small purchases in
convenience stores and other shops.

■ Airports

There are two international airports in the area. One is Narita, conveniently linked by special trains called the Narita Express or the Keisei Skyliner. You need to buy a ticket before getting on these trains. Tokyo's other airport, Haneda, is within the city itself. It used to offer mainly domestic flights, but has expanded to include international flights to destinations all over the world. The Keikyu Airport Line, departing from Shinagawa Station, is a convenient way to get there.

Haneda Airport
International
Passenger Terminal

■ Buses

Although train and subway lines run throughout the city, carrying you to numerous destinations in Tokyo and its surrounding suburbs, for locations not served by nearby train stations, there are also many bus lines. These are operated either by private companies or by Tokyo's metropolitan government.

Most bus lines originate at key train stations, allowing for seamless travel when you change from the train or subway to a bus route. Fewer of the signs are in English, so it's best to ask in advance about which bus you need, which destination it is headed for, and which stop you should get off at.

■ Taxis

In addition to trains, subways, and bus lines, you will find taxi services for situations where a place is too far to get to on foot or for when you have a lot of luggage. At train stations and near major buildings, you will find signs that say "Taxi Stand," often with several taxis waiting nearby for fares. Most taxis allow you to pay using credit cards, Suica or PASMO. There is also an app called *JapanTaxi* that you can download and which is linked with your credit card.

■ Crowding

In a city as large as Tokyo, with millions commuting to and from work each weekday morning and evening, it's hard to imagine how crowded the trains and subways are during rush hour—unless you experience it yourself.

In peak hours, trains are filled beyond their official capacity, so many passengers push each other as they hurry to get on or off the trains. More than 3.4 million passengers pass through Shinjuku, a major station on the west side of the city, every day. No other station in the world has such numbers of people coming and going.

If you want an amazing train experience in Japan, try one of the Shinkansen bullet trains that depart from Tokyo Station.

The bullet trains leave from Tokyo for all

Bullet Train at
Tokyo Station

points north, including Hakodate, the gateway
to the island of Hokkaido, and all points west of
Tokyo including Osaka, Hiroshima, Fukuoka,
and Kagoshima, a city in the southern part of
the island of Kyushu.

If you take the Tokaido Shinkansen, you can
ride from Tokyo to Osaka or Kyoto (a distance of
approximately 500 km) in two and a half hours,
and the service is available every 15 minutes or
so.

■ Safety

Moving around on public transportation is both
comfortable and efficient. Tokyo is relatively safe
for a large city, but there is crime everywhere
in the world, so you should still be careful. In

case of an emergency, the number for the police is 110, and the number for emergency medical services or fire is 119. There are police boxes, known as *koban*, in every neighborhood in Tokyo. Many are staffed twenty-four hours a day. Even if the officers are not good at speaking English, you will be treated nicely if you need help.

Chapter 4
Tokyo, a Cultural Kaleidoscope

Ryogoku Kokugikan (top),
Bunraku (bottom)

【東京の文化】

東京には、世界に誇る伝統文化と現代のポップカルチャーが共存しています。江戸を中心とした独自の町人文化は「化政文化」として知られ、歌舞伎や浮世絵を発展させました。また、今や「アニメ」、「漫画」、「コスプレ」という日本語は世界で市民権を得ています。下町や原宿・秋葉原、そして日本にある美術・博物館の4分の1が集まる東京を歩けば、千変万化の日本の文化を楽しめます。

● わからない語は巻末のワードリストで確認しましょう。

- □ kaleidoscope
- □ subculture
- □ neighborhood
- □ distinctive
- □ enthusiastic
- □ branch
- □ collection
- □ depict

● 主な地名および名称、固有名詞

□ Ghibli Museum	（三鷹の森）ジブリ美術館
□ Miyazaki Hayao	宮崎駿
□ Urayasu	浦安
□ shitamachi	下町
□ yagiri no watashi	矢切の渡し
□ Taishakuten	柴又帝釈天, 帝釈天 題経寺
□ Monzen-machi	門前町
□ Kabuki-za	歌舞伎座
□ Bunraku	文楽
□ Kamakura	鎌倉
□ Nikko Toshogu	日光東照宮
□ Dazaifu	太宰府（市）
□ Ueno Park	上野恩賜公園
□ Meiji Restoration	明治維新
□ National Treasure	国宝
□ Important Cultural Property	重要文化財
□ National Museum of Western Art	国立西洋美術館
□ Ryogoku Kokugikan	両国国技館

Modern culture

People have many different reasons for visiting Tokyo.

Akihabara

Coming to Tokyo for an important business meeting is one of them. However, tourists appreciate Tokyo for its mix of modern and historical culture.

These days many foreign tourists come to Japan to enjoy popular culture. Japanese subcultures like anime, manga, and cosplay are so famous abroad that places like Harajuku and Akihabara are packed with visitors from all over the world.

It's interesting to stroll through these areas to see all the creative new fashions and explore the small shops to find unique decorations or anime goods.

If you're a fan of manga, don't miss the Ghibli

Museum in Mitaka City, a suburb in the west part of Tokyo. This museum was designed by Miyazaki Hayao, the world-famous anime creator.

Also, many young visitors want to experience Tokyo Disneyland and DisneySea, one of the largest amusement parks based on Disney characters in the world. They're located in Urayasu, near Tokyo Bay. Tokyo is the best place to the enjoy modern culture of Japan.

Traditional culture

On the other hand, if you're interested in the traditional side of Japan, visit the eastern side of Tokyo. There are many traditional neighborhoods, known as *shitamachi*, where you can get a good sense of what Tokyo was like in the past. *Shitamachi* districts, like Asakusa, can be found along the Sumida-gawa River, or in areas like Kanda, Tabata and their vicinity.

■ The Sumida-gawa River

From Ryogoku to Asakusa, and from Ryogoku to Tsukishima, try walking along the Sumida-gawa River, where you will feel the atmosphere of the Edo period, when the townspeople's houses and shops stretched along this river.

Just like a kaleidoscope, the river's waves have been reflecting lights and shadows of countless stories featured in ukiyo-e, Kabuki, and even modern manga, reflecting 400 years of life in Edo and Tokyo.

■ The Edo-gawa River

If you want to go a little farther north, follow the Edo-gawa River. There, you can see boats called *yagiri no watashi*, a type of flat-bottomed boat

Yagiri no watashi

that has been used to ferry people from one side of the river to the other for more than 400 years. These boats are still used today, and are popular with tourists who cherish both the views and the memories.

■ Shibamata

On the eastern side of the river is the Shibamata neighborhood, at the center of

Taishakuten

which is a Buddhist temple called Taishakuten. It was constructed in 1609. Past Taishakuten is the Monzen-machi neighborhood, which has a shopping street that has kept its distinctive atmosphere from olden times.

Kabuki and Bunraku

Experiencing Kabuki, or Japanese-style opera, is another fantastic experience. If you'd like to

Kabuki-za

see a performance, visit the Kabuki-za, located in Higashi-ginza, which is part of the Ginza district. Kabuki plays capture the audience's enthusiastic attention with distinctive rhythms, voice intonations, and theatrical postures. Kabuki originated in the Osaka and Kyoto area during the Edo period and was later brought to Edo, along with puppet theater called Bunraku.

Kabuki was considered scandalous during the Edo period, and the government prohibited women from acting in Kabuki plays. Therefore, to this day, all the actors on stage, even the ones in women's roles, are male. You can enjoy

Kabuki with an English audio guide in the Kabuki-za, as well as at the National Theater, where you can enjoy also Bunraku. The National Theater is located on the western side of the Imperial Palace.

Experiencing history near Tokyo

Tokyo is not an ancient city like Rome. While the best places to experience Japanese history from the ancient period are Kyoto and Nara,

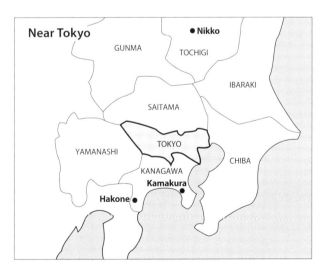

they are located 500 km west of Tokyo. However, Kamakura and Nikko are conveniently located nearby.

Kamakura was the headquarters of the military government between 1192 and 1333, so it is full of ancient shrines, temples, and other historical places of interest.

There is a gorgeous shrine complex with beautiful mountains, lakes, and forests in Nikko. A shrine called Nikko Toshogu was built for Tokugawa Ieyasu, the first shogun, in the seventeenth century. Convenient train services are available for getting to both Kamakura and Nikko. Hakone is another recommendation, where you can enjoy a mountainous resort environment at the foot of Mt. Fuji.

Museums in Tokyo

■ National museums

If you don't have enough time to visit places

outside of Tokyo, you can get a good sense of the country's past from its museums. Indeed, there are countless museums in Tokyo.

One of the best is the National Museum. There are also branches of the National Museum located in Kyoto, Nara, and in a town called Dazaifu in Kyushu, each with a collection of historic remains and works of art from Japan, Asia, and around the world.

Of the four National Museums, the one in Ueno Park has the largest collection. Established in 1872, just four years after the Meiji Restoration, the museum's collection of 110,000 pieces includes 87 National Treasures

The National Museum of Western Art

and 634 Important Cultural Properties. Near the National Museum in Ueno, there are other interesting museums as well. The National Museum of Western Art not only has a wonderful collection, but the building was designed by the famous French architect Le Corbusier.

■ The Edo-Tokyo Museum

If you want to experience the specific history of Tokyo, try the Edo-Tokyo Museum, which is located near Ryogoku Station. This museum is a unique and entertaining space in which to experience and look back on the city, from its historical origin as Edo to its present existence as modern Tokyo. Many of its exhibits are 3D reproductions of life as it was lived in olden times, depicting scenes around town.

Proceeding to modern times, we can see the transformation of people's lives and how they survived the hardships of World War Two, for instance. The museum offers unparalleled insights into this dynamic city, based on exhibits that bring its historical roots to life in an entertaining and understandable manner.

■ Tokyo's unique museums

Besides the major museums, there are some unique museums in Tokyo. For example, at the Nezu Museum, located in Aoyama, you can enjoy an antique collection in a traditional atmosphere. Near Harajuku, there is a museum called the Ota Memorial Museum of Art, which exhibits marvelous ukiyo-e collections. And in Fukagawa, there is a museum called the Fukagawa Edo Museum, which has exhibits on life in Tokyo during the Edo period. This museum is located just beside a charming traditional Japanese garden called Kiyosumi Park, which was the home of a feudal lord during the Edo period. Of course, these are just three examples of many.

Unique Museums in Tokyo

- Samurai Museum (Shinjuku)

- Fire Museum (Yotsuya)

- Meguro Parasitological Museum (Meguro)

- The Sumida Hokusai Museum (Sumida)

- National Museum of Emerging Science and Innovation Miraikan (Koto)

Katsushika Hokusai "The Great Wave off Kanagawa"

- Subway Museum (Edogawa)

- Museum of Yebisu Beer (Ebisu)

- Edo-Tokyo Open Air Architectural Museum (Koganei City)

Sports

Tokyo is not only a cultural and economic hub; it is also the center of professional sports in Japan. From professional baseball to football, there are many sporting events being held throughout the

Greater Tokyo Area. For example, Tokyo Dome, near Koraku-en Station, has professional baseball games from spring to autumn. Including Tokyo Dome, there are five professional baseball stadiums in the downtown and its suburbs.

As for traditional sports, Japanese people have been enjoying sumo wrestling since the ancient era. Originally sumo was an event to celebrate the harvest in front of the gods. Near the Edo-Tokyo Museum, there is a stadium called the Ryogoku Kokugikan, where sumo matches take place in January, May, and September.

Chapter 5
Tokyo, a Food Lover's Paradise

Kaiten-zushi (top),
Ramen (bottom)

【東京の食】

目まぐるしい日常を過ごす東京の人々は、友人との食事や仕事終わりの一杯をゆっくり楽しみます。居酒屋でお酒やおつまみを味わい、締めにラーメン屋へ。フレンチや中華など、さまざまな国の料理店もあります。江戸時代にはファストフードだった寿司やそばは、日本食の代表として海外でも人気です。疲れた日には、デパ地下で美味しいお惣菜とスイーツを買って帰るのもいいですね。

●わからない語は巻末のワードリストで確認しましょう。

☐ Tokyoite	☐ specialize	☐ cuisine
☐ equivalent	☐ décor	☐ ingredient
☐ broth	☐ basement	

●主な地名および名称、固有名詞

☐ izakaya	居酒屋
☐ yakitori	焼き鳥
☐ yokocho	横丁
☐ sake	日本酒
☐ shochu	焼酎
☐ joren	常連
☐ kishimen	きしめん
☐ World Heritage	世界遺産
☐ kaiten-zushi	回転寿司
☐ nigiri-zushi	握り寿司
☐ edomae	江戸前
☐ atsukan	熱燗，燗酒
☐ yatai	屋台
☐ mori-soba	盛りそば
☐ tempura	天ぷら
☐ Toyosu Fish Market	豊洲市場
☐ Tsukiji Fish Market	築地市場
☐ depa-chika	デパ地下

Eating out

Tokyoites love to eat out, partly because life there is so fast-paced, and it's very common for friends and coworkers to meet for dinner or drinks after work. From the traditional Japanese-style pub called *izakaya* to the exclusive international restaurants, practically every food in the world is available in Tokyo.

■ Specialization

First of all, you need to know that many of the best Japanese restaurants specialize in just one kind of dish. For example, one popular type of restaurant specializes in *yakitori*, grilled chicken skewered on a bamboo stick. These restaurants are called *yakitori-ya*. Similarly, *soba-ya* usually sell only soba, and *ramen-ya* sell only ramen.

■ International cuisines

Of course, from French to Chinese, and from Middle-Eastern to Mexican, you can enjoy many international cuisines in Tokyo as well. And after eating, you will find many bars and drinking places in the major centers.

■ Finding traditional food

Tokyo developed its eating culture during the Edo period. Many well-known types of restaurants, including soba noodle shops and sushi bars, can be traced back to the days of the samurai.

To find a taste of traditional Tokyo, look for narrow streets near business centers. Such streets are called *yokocho*. Walking through a *yokocho* often feels like walking through Tokyo fifty years ago.

And you will discover many small, traditional restaurants and drinking places there, such as *izakaya*.

■ *Izakaya*

In Western countries hardworking office staff might stop at a bar or pub on their way home from a day's work, sharing a drink and light snacks with coworkers. In Japan, the equivalent is an *izakaya*, and here, too, the journey home is pleasantly interrupted.

An *izakaya* will typically have traditional décor, usually with a wooden counter for those drinking alone or in pairs. There are also tables and chairs for those in groups, and sometimes straw tatami mats, some of which will have sunken floors under the tables so that people can comfortably stretch out their legs.

The selection of beverages is generally fairly broad and normally includes beer on tap. Some *izakaya* specialize in Japanese sake, and others in *shochu* (a distilled drink made from potatoes, rye, or other ingredients, and with an alcohol content of 25 to 30 percent). If you go to *izakaya* regularly, you may become known as a *joren* (regular customer), encountering other regulars and falling easily into post-work conversations.

■ Ramen noodle shops

Whether for a quick bite of lunch or a final meal at the end of a pleasant evening out drinking with friends, ramen is one of Japan's most popular noodle dishes, served in a hot bowl of broth and complemented by a variety of toppings. With a consistency different from Japan's other traditional noodles, such as udon, soba, *kishimen*, or *somen*, ramen noodles have a slightly tougher texture. There are four main varieties of ramen, often associated with a particular region of Japan. In Tokyo, you can enjoy all kinds of ramen from Kyushu's pork broth noodles to Hokkaido's miso flavor, as well as original Tokyo varieties.

■ *Kaiten-zushi*

Sushi bars are known for being very expensive, but if you want to enjoy sushi for a reasonable price, try a conveyor-belt sushi restaurant. When Japanese cuisine achieved World Heritage status, the idea of conveyor-belt sushi restaurants was likely not a reason that Japanese food was added to the list. While it might not be as good as the traditional sushi that helped Japanese cuisine to gain international recognition, *kaiten-zushi* is a uniquely Japanese food experience.

Traditionally, stepping into a sushi restaurant usually meant being seated at a big wooden counter and talking with the chef as you watched your sushi being prepared piece by piece. Unfortunately, this experience was also so expensive that it was reserved for special occasions or the wealthy, and it was not easy for ordinary people to enjoy sushi in their everyday life.

Kaiten-zushi's revolving array of sushi plates lets customers choose their favorite sushi for an affordable price, bringing Japan's traditional vinegared rice and raw fish to more of Japan's population.

■ *Nigiri-zushi*

The sushi with a slice of fish on top of rice that you see at sushi bars or *kaiten-zushi* shops is called *nigiri-zushi*. This style of sushi is called *edomae* (Edo style) because it started as a snack for Edo's townspeople, who ate it at small portable sushi stands. At that time, it was not a main meal. In the early twentieth century, sushi gradually became a common dish for eating out. Sake is good with sushi, particularly *atsukan*, or hot sake, which is especially good in winter.

■ Noodles

Soba, or buckwheat noodles, also became

popular during the Edo period. Soba was served at soba restaurants or, like sushi, at portable eating stands called *yatai*.

Now there are many soba restaurants in Tokyo. There are two ways of eating soba. One is to order soba noodles in broth. This is served like ramen with various ingredients. The other way is to order *mori-soba*, or cold soba. Sometimes, people order cold soba with tempura. These days, soba has become popular among Westerners because it is relatively healthy even though it is fried.

Fish market

A visit to the Toyosu Fish Market is an excellent way to appreciate Tokyo's food culture. Products including fish, fruit, and vegetables are sold at this huge wholesale market. It is a replacement for the Tsukiji Fish Market, which closed in 2018. There are many restaurants and food-related shops around both markets that make the areas very popular with tourists.

Department store basements

Tokyo's department store basements are another excellent way to get a taste of the city's most delicious foods. They are known as *depa-chika* (a shortened version of the Japanese word for "department store basement"). There you can purchase a wide variety of foods and alcoholic drinks from Japan and around the world, including traditional Japanese and Western sweets. The *depa-chika* floor of a department store is also one of the best places to find ingredients for traditional Japanese cuisine.

Because they are filled with ready-to-eat foods that are prepared to high standards, *depa-chika* are a popular place for busy people to purchase main dishes for dinner. Seasonal gifts, too, are appreciated when they have been bought and sent from the *depa-chika* of a well-known department store.

There are many department stores in Tokyo. They are concentrated in areas of the city where many people gather, such as in Ginza and Nihonbashi, and also near stations with large numbers of commuters passing through, including Shinjuku, Shibuya, Ikebukuro, and Ueno.

Department stores embody the essence of service found only in Japan, where the spirit of the nation's traditional hospitality can be observed in the way each customer is taken care of by highly-trained and extremely courteous staff.

This is one reason that department stores have become popular destination spots for foreign visitors to Japan.

Chapter 6
Tokyo, Cities Within a City

Rainbow Bridge (top),
Ginza 4-chome (bottom)

【東京のまち歩き】

地上と地下に鉄道路線が張り巡らされている東京。その中心部を移動するなら、地下鉄や私鉄にもアクセスしやすいJRの山手線が便利です。都心をぐるりと一周する山手線の駅周辺はエリアごとの特色があり、一駅の間だけ歩いてみても異なる風景や雰囲気を楽しむことができます。p.36–37のマップを参照しながら、英語でまち歩きに出かけてみませんか？

●わからない語は巻末のワードリストで確認しましょう。

☐ artifact	☐ stroll	☐ fortress
☐ surround	☐ district	☐ luxurious
☐ affordable	☐ boulevard	

●主な地名および名称、固有名詞

☐ Nijubashi Bridge	二重橋
☐ Showa Emperor	昭和天皇
☐ Imperial Palace East Garden	皇居東御苑
☐ Sakuradamon Gate	桜田門
☐ Hama Rikyu Detached Palace	浜離宮恩賜庭園
☐ Imperial Household Agency	宮内庁
☐ Bodhisattva Kannon	観音菩薩（観世音菩薩）
☐ Naito-Shinjuku	内藤新宿
☐ Hachiko	（忠犬）ハチ公
☐ Ministry of Defence	防衛省
☐ Takeshita-dori Street	竹下通り
☐ Meiji-jingu Shrine	明治神宮
☐ Kanda Myojin Shrine	神田明神
☐ Asakusa-bashi Bridge	浅草橋
☐ Ameyoko	アメ横
☐ Yancsen	谷根千
☐ Somei-Yoshino	ソメイヨシノ
☐ Shiba Imperial Villa	旧芝離宮恩賜庭園

Almost all the main areas of Tokyo are found on the edge of or inside the circle formed by the Yamanote Line. To experience the heart of Tokyo, and Japan itself, let's start with the area of the Imperial Palace, which is located near Tokyo Station.

Around the Imperial Palace (Edo Castle)

■ Imperial Palace (Edo Castle)

The present-day Imperial Palace was known in the olden days as Edo Castle, and it is where the Edo-based military shogunate that ruled over Japan until 1868 was located. There was once a large fortress on the castle grounds, but it burned down in fires during the Edo period.

Central Tower of Edo Castle

■ Palace moats

Now this area is home to the Imperial Palace and is where the emperor resides. From the time it was constructed, the castle was surrounded for protection by the Inner and Outer Moats, and in the past, the residences of many feudal lords and the homes of relatively high-ranking samurai were located between them. Today, many historical sites and artifacts have been preserved in the area, and there is a popular 5-kilometer jogging course around the Outer Moat.

■ Nijubashi Bridge

Nijubashi Bridge is located on the main, front side of the Imperial Palace. There is a double-arched bridge nearby (the Seimon Ishibashi) that many visitors mistake for it, but the real Nijubashi is a single-arched bridge located behind this structure.

The real Nijubashi was originally built in 1614 and then rebuilt in 1964. On August 15,

Seimon Ishibashi

1945, when the Showa Emperor's unconditional surrender speech, which ended World War Two, was broadcast over the radio, thousands of citizens gathered in the large area in front of the bridge to hear the broadcast. Many were overcome with grief and astonishment when they heard the Emperor's own voice proclaiming Japan's surrender.

■ The gates of Edo Castle

The Otemon Gate faces east and was considered to be the main gate of the castle. If you enter the palace grounds from here, you can see the stone foundations of Edo Castle as you walk through. Nowadays, the inner area of the old castle is called the Imperial Palace East Gardens. Although the Imperial Palace itself is not open to the public, tourists can enjoy strolling through this beautiful green oasis in the center of the city. One of the most popular areas is the Ninomaru Teien, a traditional Japanese garden.

Also, do not forget to see the Sakuradamon Gate, which is located at the south end of where Edo Castle was. This spot is famous as the place where a chief minister of the Tokugawa Shogunate was assassinated one snowy day in March of 1860. This event was one of the major incidents that led to the fall of the Tokugawa Shogunate.

Another important gate is the Tayasumon Gate, which was constructed in 1638. Located at the northern end of the Edo Castle remains, this entrance lets you enter Kitanomaru Park and contains the impressive foundations remaining from the Kitanomaru fortress tower.

In addition, the park has an unusually broad lawn surrounded by wooded paths, allowing for a stress-free picnic or stroll when the weather is good.

Tokyo Station and surrounding area

■ Tokyo Station

From the Nijubashi area, a wide road lined with beautiful pine trees leads you to Tokyo Station, the city's most important transportation hub.

Tokyo Station

This distinctive red brick building faces the Imperial Palace and was built in 1914. The present-day reconstruction was modeled on that building after its destruction during World War Two. The western side of this red-brick station building is referred to as the Marunouchi Entrance, and the opposite, eastern side, is called the Yaesu Entrance.

Tokyo Station has evolved into a truly enormous transportation facility with underground tracks, above-ground lines, the Shinkansen bullet train terminals, and several subway lines. There is also a huge shopping arcade underneath it.

■ Otemachi and Nihonbashi

The northern side of the Marunouchi Entrance is called Otemachi, and it is the financial center of Tokyo. Many of Japan's biggest companies have their headquarters there.

The area on the eastern side, where the bullet train terminal is located, is called Nihonbashi.

Hiroshige "Nihonbashi, Morning Scene"

It is named for the famous Nihonbashi Bridge. It was built in 1603, and was constructed out of wood. In order to connect the new capital with the rest of Japan, Tokugawa Ieyasu, who founded the military shogunate, ordered that five major roads be built.

These five roads to and from the capital would all meet in Nihonbashi, and from that time to the present, Nihonbashi has served as mile zero for any location in Japan. The present bridge was built in 1911.

Around this bridge is one of the major shopping hubs, with several department stores and countless commercial buildings. Some of

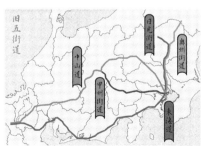

The Gokaido, the five highways leading to Edo

these stores trace their origins back to the Edo period, when this area was the commercial center of the country. Actually, during the Edo period, Nihonbashi was also a lively business district for the townspeople, as Tokyo's fish market was originally located there. There are many old shops in Nihonbashi selling traditional foodstuffs and goods that date back to the days of the old fish market.

Around Ginza

■ Ginza

It goes without saying that Ginza is known the world over as Tokyo's premier shopping district. Department stores, boutiques, and shops selling globally recognized brand-name goods line the main street, Chuo-dori, while the alleys and side streets are lined with the bright signs of countless restaurants, nightclubs, and other entertainment spots.

Ginza's name originates in the silver coins (*gin* is the Japanese word for silver) that were minted there during the Edo period.

■ Shinbashi and Yurakucho

To the south of Tokyo Station past the southern tip of Ginza, there are two stations named Shinbashi and Yurakucho. The area between them is filled with small alleys containing countless drinking spots and restaurants. In contrast to the upscale clubs of Ginza, Shinbashi and Yurakucho are known as casual, reasonably priced spots for salaried workers to drink in.

Close to Shinbashi in the direction of Tokyo Bay is an area called Shiodome. The Hama Rikyu Detached Palace is a must-see traditional garden near the heart of Tokyo. When it was constructed in 1654, it jutted into Edo Bay with

Hama Rikyu Detached Palace

its fortress-like stone embankment. Later the garden became the Detached Palace and is now part of the Imperial Household Agency. It is open to the public under the administration of the Tokyo city government.

■ Odaiba

Odaiba is one of the most modern and scenic parts of Tokyo, and it is an easy trip from Shinbashi on the new elevated train called the Yurikamome Line. The rubber-wheeled train glides quietly over the Rainbow Bridge, a picturesque suspension bridge, to the expanding landfill islands where Odaiba is located. In the past, Odaiba was a fortress that protected Edo from foreign ships. However, it is now known for its shopping complexes and convention centers.

■ Marunouchi

Walking north in the Marunouchi area between Yurakucho and Tokyo Station, you will notice the buildings that made this district truly representative of Tokyo's stately post-war business atmosphere. The area has been transformed in recent years, though, with numerous high-end boutiques, shops, and restaurants.

Around Asakusa

■ Asakusa

One of the most popular tourist destinations in Tokyo today is the old neighborhood of Asakusa. It has been well known since the Edo period as an entertainment district with playhouses and pleasure quarter facilities lining its narrow alleys. It also prospered due to its proximity to Senso-ji Temple, with its famous gate, hanging red lantern, and crowded street lined with stalls selling food and handicrafts.

Senso-ji Temple is the oldest Buddhist temple in Tokyo, dating back to AD 645. The temple houses a statue of the Bodhisattva Kannon, which, according to legend, was discovered by

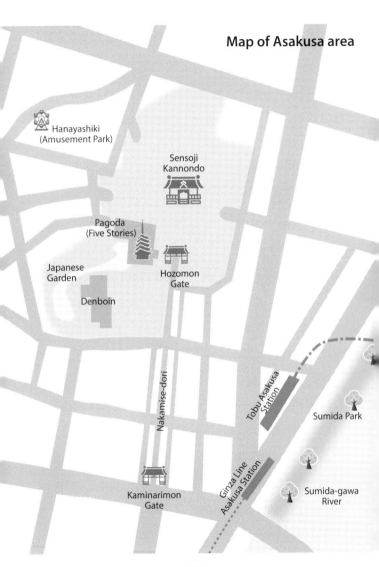

Map of Asakusa area

Hanayashiki
(Amusement Park)

Sensoji
Kannondo

Pagoda
(Five Stories)

Japanese
Garden

Hozomon
Gate

Denboin

Nakamise-dori

Tobu Asakusa
Station

Sumida Park

Kaminarimon
Gate

Ginza Line
Asakusa Station

Sumida-gawa
River

fishermen in the nearby Sumida-gawa River. Kannon is believed to be a compassionate, enlightened being devoted to helping all humans reach enlightenment.

Today, the area surrounding Senso-ji Temple is a popular destination for visitors from overseas, who are attracted in part by the chance to buy Japanese souvenirs at reasonable prices while reveling in the historic atmosphere of a bustling street-stall market, with restaurants, folk-craft shops, and the feel of a quaint entertainment district.

■ Kappabashi

Very close to Asakusa is a shopping district called Kappabashi, which is famous for its many shops selling cooking utensils and goods used in the restaurant business. In recent years, Japanese cuisine has received global recognition and been added to UNESCO's Lists of Intangible Cultural Heritage.

Many Japanese shoppers, as well as those from abroad, visit the Kappabashi district in search of the unique

Plastic food models

utensils used to prepare Japanese dishes, including distinctive Japanese kitchen knives.

Another popular item available in Kappabashi is the plastic food models you may have seen in restaurant display windows giving passersby a preview of what can be ordered inside.

■ The Sumida-gawa River

If you're heading from Asakusa to Tsukishima through Fukagawa and Ryogoku, it is a good idea to walk along the Sumida-gawa River. Or if you would prefer a cruise, there are boat services too.

It was once an area crowded with Edo's craftspeople, and the Sumida-gawa River was crowded with boats transporting people and

goods. It was a lively, bustling area of Edo.

■ Oshiage

Not far from the Asakusa
area, in a neighborhood
called Oshiage, is the
world's tallest communi-

Tokyo Skytree

cations tower. Known as the Tokyo Skytree, it
is an impressive 634 meters tall. Completed in
2012 and opened with a shopping mall at its
base, the Skytree offers an unparalleled view
from its observation deck, not only of the whole
of metropolitan Tokyo, but of the surrounding
prefectures as well.

Shinjuku and vicinity

■ Shinjuku

There are many major train stations along the
Yamanote Line on the western side of Tokyo,
but Shinjuku is by far the largest. During the

Edo period, it was an overnight lodging area for travelers approaching or leaving the capital, and it was known as Naito-Shinjuku.

Today, Shinjuku is split in two by the Yamanote Line. Its western side is known as *Fukutoshin* ("the second core of the city"), and it houses Tokyo's city hall and many high-rise hotels and office buildings. The eastern side of Shinjuku is largely an entertainment and shopping district. Along with other areas such as Ginza and Shibuya, Shinjuku is one of the key shopping areas in Tokyo.

In particular, Kabuki-cho is known as Japan's largest nightlife entertainment area, somewhat similar to Times Square in New York City.

Tokyo's city hall

■ The Golden-Gai

Beside Kabuki-cho is an area known as the Golden-Gai. Packed with tiny bars and restaurants, it feels a little like stepping back in time to the latter part of the Showa era of the 1950s through the 1970s. It has long been loved by not only salaried workers stopping in for a drink on the way home, but also by artists, authors, and other cultured intellectuals. A similar area, called Omoide-yokocho, can be found in the northwestern corner of the Shinjuku Station area. Shops there featuring such fare as *yakitori* chicken skewers and ramen noodles are nestled into tiny spaces next to each other.

■ Shin-Okubo

The next station on the Yamanote Line to the north of Shinjuku is called Shin-Okubo. Situated around Shin-Okubo Station is Tokyo's largest concentration of Korean shops, selling food and a full range of goods, and in addition to the many Korean restaurants, there are Chinese, Indian, and numerous other Asian spots where you can enjoy a full range of Asian culinary delights.

■ Shinjuku Gyoen

After experiencing the busy city life, why not visit Shinjuku Gyoen Park, which originated during the Meiji period as an agricultural/ horticultural testing center? It was opened to the public after World War Two. This park includes not only a traditional Japanese garden but French- and British-style gardens too.

Around Shibuya and Roppongi

■ Shibuya

Continuing to follow the Yamanote Line, we come to Shibuya. Shibuya Station is the third station south of Shinjuku. Shibuya was once on the outskirts of Edo, and is known for its vibrant youth culture. It has also evolved into a commercial center known as a hot spot for emerging trends.

Shibuya is famous for its constant flow of people. The intersection at the northwest side of the station is known not only in Japan but abroad, and is famous for the enormous crowds crossing to and from the entertainment and shopping districts nearby.

■ Hachiko

The bronze statue of a dog named Hachiko at the station exit on this side is also famous, as it serves as a convenient meeting spot for

Hachiko

Shibuya Intersection

friends to find each other. The 2009 film starring Richard Gere called *Hachi: A Dog's Tale* took its name and inspiration from the real-life story of the dog memorialized near the station.

Ever faithful to its owner, Hachi would greet a university professor each day on his commute home to Shibuya Station. In 1925, when the professor unexpectedly passed away and did not return, Hachiko patiently continued coming to the station every day for nine years!

Near Shibuya, there are many fashionable, international neighborhoods like Daikan-yama, Ebisu, and Hiroo. These areas are home to large numbers of foreigners working for global firms.

■ Roppongi

Roppongi is just a short bus ride from Shibuya, or if you want to use the train, take the Yamanote Line to Ebisu and change to the subway Hibiya Line. Roppongi is the second station after Hiroo.

Roppongi is Tokyo's most famous party spot, well known for its many bars and unique restaurants with cuisine from around the world, and is frequented by many foreign residents and tourists.

As the crossing point for both the subway Oedo and the Hibiya Lines, this is an easily accessible area, and you can find a number of international firms and foreign embassies within easy reach of Roppongi Station.

In the olden days, this was an area where many *daimyo*, or local lords, maintained their residences in Tokyo, as did other members of the samurai class. Later, in the years preceding World War Two, the district was home to a number of military bases and facilities, and until recently the Ministry of Defense maintained its headquarters there as well. Traces of the past have largely disappeared, however, and Roppongi has been transformed due to the construction of a huge shopping and hotel complex called Tokyo Midtown. On the south side of the famous Roppongi Crossing, an intersection in front of the station, is Roppongi Hills, which is also crammed with luxurious shops, restaurants, and hotels.

■ Tokyo Tower

Convenient to Roppongi, Tokyo Tower, which was modeled after the Eiffel Tower in Paris, was completed in 1958. It was the tallest free-standing tower in the world at the time. With two observation decks accessible for public viewing at 150 and 250 meters high respectively, Tokyo Tower remains a very popular tourist destination for both Japanese and foreign visitors.

above: Eiffel Tower
below: Tokyo Tower

■ Azabu-juban

Azabu-juban is another interesting spot that should not be missed. It is a casual shopping and dining neighborhood to the east of Roppongi. Historically, this is where the *daimyo* of the Sendai feudal domain maintained their residence during the Edo period.

These days, one finds the streets of Azabu-juban filled with families and couples out for a stroll, shopping in small shops and dining in small, distinctive restaurants that provide a contrast to the bustling atmosphere in Roppongi, just a ten-minute walk away.

Harajuku, Omote-sando, and Aoyama

■ Harajuku

Recognized globally as a Mecca for youth fashion, Harajuku attracts people from around the world to visit and shop in its countless boutiques.

In the neighborhood surrounding Takeshita-dori Street, near the east exit of Harajuku Station, shops sell creative, trendsetting clothing and accessories, all at reasonable prices. It was in the 1990s that Harajuku and Akihabara gave birth to trends that have become known around the world, such as the popular *otaku* subcultures of anime and cosplay.

Harajuku is just a short walk from Shibuya. In the other direction, there is a large, famous Shinto shrine called Meiji-jingu, which is located deep in a wooded area that stretches from the western side of Harajuku Station. This shrine itself is relatively new, as it was built in 1920 to

Meij-jingu Shrine

memorialize the Empress and Emperor Meiji. However, the forest and buildings create a highly traditional atmosphere.

■ Omote-sando

The wide, tree-lined boulevard stretching majestically from Aoyama-dori Street to the entrance of Meiji-jingu Shrine is known as Omote-sando.

Both sides of the boulevard are lined with attractive, upscale storefronts, and numerous side streets leading off the main avenue are home to stylish shops, boutiques, and restaurants. The distinctive feel and ambiance of the neighborhood have led to Omote-sando's well-earned reputation as a place where Tokyo residents can enjoy an unhurried and refined city culture.

■ Aoyama

The Aoyama district is one of the city's most elegant areas. Filled with boutiques and high-class dining options, this is the place to go if you want luxury goods from around the world.

The main street, Aoyama-dori, connected Shibuya with Edo Castle and was known as the location of the official residences of powerful *daimyo* during the Edo period.

Kanda and Akihabara

■ Kanda

Like Shinbashi, Kanda is a salaried worker's area, and is an interesting place for foreign visitors to stroll through at night. There are countless affordable *izakaya*, sushi restaurants, and ramen shops, where people stop after work for a drink or meal.

Kanda originally developed around the Kanda Myojin Shrine. Kanda is also known for the Yushima-Seido, which was built as a university for the study of Confucianism in 1690.

One of the characteristics of this area is used

Yasukuni-jinja

bookstores. Along Yasukuni-dori Street, there are many shops selling antique books, some of which are centuries old.

After passing through the antique bookshop area to the west, there is a shrine called Yasukuni-jinja, which has a huge *torii*, or gate. This shrine was built as a war memorial. It is also politically controversial as many war criminals from World War Two were also enshrined there.

■ Akihabara

If you stroll north from Kanda for a few minutes, you will come to Akihabara, the world's largest electronics district, where the streets are lined with retail stores large and small, selling general household appliances and electronic goods. As we have already mentioned, Akihabara is also famous as the center of *otaku* culture.

From Akihabara, traveling to the next station on the Sobu Line brings you to the Asakusa-bashi area. In the Edo period, there was a bridge called Asakusa-bashi Bridge on the moat of Edo Castle in this area. If you go out of the station's east exit, you can find small shops and wholesalers selling Japan's traditional dolls lining the streets of the neighborhood.

Ueno and "Yanesen"

■ Ameyoko

Ueno Station was developed as a terminal for trains from the northern part of Japan. In the south part of the lively Ueno area is a traditional marketplace called Ameyoko. In the aftermath of Tokyo's destruction by bombing during World War Two, a black-market shopping street crowded with stalls selling commodities and daily goods sprang up. This gave rise to the bustling shopping area still popular today.

Ameyoko

Until not long ago the street was lined with countless shops selling ingredients for Japanese cuisine, but in recent years, many shops catering to customers looking for goods and foodstuffs from other Asian countries have appeared, and the neighborhood is now a more diverse place. Around Ameyoko, there are also many Japanese-style stand-up bars and casual traditional restaurants.

■ Ueno Park

Ueno Park, on the west side of the station, is home to many museums, as well as the Shinobazu Pond, which dates from the seventeenth century. At the bottom of the hill,

Shinobazu Pond

near the Shinobazu Pond, is the Ueno Zoo.

Ueno Park was once part of Kan'ei-ji Temple, which was used by the shoguns. Kan'ei-ji can still be visited on the northern hill of Ueno Park, and remains a place where you can enjoy the silence of old Edo. Ueno Park is also one of the most famous places for enjoying cherry blossoms in late March or early April.

■ Yanesen

To the north of Ueno Park, along Shinobazu-dori Street, there are neighborhoods called Yanaka, Nezu, and Sendagi. People often refer to them as "Ya-ne-sen," after the first sounds in each of their names.

If you are using the Yamanote Line, get off at Nippori Station and walk along the boulevard heading west to Yanaka. Here, on both sides of the street and in the nearby side alleys, you will find craftspeople making traditional tatami mats, antique shops, and small restaurants specializing in what is sometimes called "Japanese tapas"—many varieties of folksy food served on small dishes.

This neighborhood is well worth a leisurely exploration, as the "Yanaka Ginza" has retained a retro-type feel of the good old days of traditional Tokyo.

Yanaka Ginza

Walking to the south of Yanaka is a neighborhood known as Nezu. Here many Buddhist temples from olden times can be found. These provide a tranquil, serene atmosphere far different from the bustle of the big city. Strolling even farther south from Nezu, you come to Ueno Park again.

A few minutes' walk from Nippori Station, there is a large cemetery in the Yanaka neighborhood known as Yanaka Reien. It is one of the best places in Tokyo to view cherry blossoms in the spring.

Around Ikebukuro and Sugamo

■ Ikebukuro

Ikebukuro is an important transit point for many people commuting into central Tokyo. With two big department stores sandwiching the station, Ikebukuro is a shopper's paradise. Together with the other popular core areas of

Shibuya and Shinjuku, also on the western side of central Tokyo, Ikebukuro is a distinctive part of the city, linked closely to the others by the Yamanote Line.

■ Sugamo

The third station to the east of Ikebukuro on the Yamanote Line is Sugamo. It was just a quiet village during the Edo period but has evolved into the vibrant neighborhood it is today. Around Kogan-ji Temple, a shopping street has grown up where many old-fashioned goods, Japanese sweets, and fashionable clothing geared to the elderly are sold. The area has become known as "Harajuku for Grannies."

■ Somei-cho

Located next to Sugamo is a neighborhood called Somei-cho, which takes its name from a historic village of the same name. It was in this village that the Somei-Yoshino cherry tree was developed. Known for their beauty the

Somei-Yoshino

world over, Somei-Yoshino trees were the ones donated to Washington, D.C., more than a century ago, gracing the Jefferson Memorial and Tidal Basin area with stunning blossoms each spring. Don't forget to visit a beautiful Japanese garden called Rikugi-en near there. This traditional garden was created in 1695 for a powerful supporter of the Tokugawa shogunate.

Shinagawa and Hamamatsu-cho

■ Shinagawa

At the southern edge of the Yamanote Line, there is another train terminal called Shinagawa. Bullet trains heading for western Japan stop at this station. Shinagawa was the first overnight stopping point during the journey from Edo to the ancient capital of Kyoto. Most travelers along the old Tokaido road connecting Edo and Kyoto made the journey on foot, taking about two weeks to complete the trip.

As there were fifty-three stations offering meals and lodging, there was flexibility regarding when and where to stop, depending on the weather and how much progress had been made each day.

These days Shinagawa is a bustling business district. Moreover, Shinagawa will be the starting point for the maglev route that will eventually connect Tokyo and Osaka, traveling at the astonishing speed of 570 kilometers per hour.

■ Hamamatsu-cho

Head back toward Tokyo Station from Shinagawa and visit one of Tokyo's most beautiful public gardens, the former Shiba Imperial Villa, which is located a short distance from Hamamatsu-cho Station on the Yamanote Line.

Not long after Edo became the capital, this area was reclaimed from Edo Bay, and the gardens originally had a beach along the shore. In 1678 the property became the official residence of a retainer of the ruling Tokugawa family, and over the next 200 years, although it changed ownership several times, it was maintained as a classical Edo-period Japanese garden. With a large central pond, bridges, a picnic area, and a wisteria trellis, these gardens are an oasis surrounded by shining skyscrapers and are not to be missed.

Another attraction around Hamamatsu-cho is Zojo-ji Temple near Tokyo Tower, which has

Zojo-ji Temple

a remarkable history, having been founded in 1393. After moving to the current location, this temple became the family temple of the Tokugawa clan. It has a stunning main gate, built in 1622, that has survived fires, earthquakes, and other disasters.

Chapter 7
Tokyo, the Priceless Inheritance of Edo Castle

Kagurazaka (top),
Remains of Edo Castle (bottom)

【江戸城について】

その地名の由来となった江戸氏の居館跡に、太田道灌が1457年に築いたのが江戸城です。道灌暗殺後、後北条氏の支配を経て、1590年に徳川家康が入城しました。1603年の江戸開府後、数十年にわたる大規模な城郭の拡張や道路・河川整備が行われ、江戸は世界有数の大都市へと発展を遂げます。1868年に開城、翌年に明治天皇が移り皇居となりましたが、今日も周辺各所にその名残をとどめています。

●わからない語は巻末のワードリストで確認しましょう。

- ☐ overwhelm
- ☐ magnificent
- ☐ bureaucrat
- ☐ administrative
- ☐ merchant
- ☐ swampland
- ☐ acquire
- ☐ inheritance

●主な地名および名称、固有名詞

☐ Kagurazaka	神楽坂
☐ Ushigome Gate	牛込門
☐ Omote	表
☐ Oku	奥
☐ O-oku	大奥
☐ Yamanote	山の手
☐ Shitamachi	下町

The road to the castle

By the late 1600s, the basic layout of modern-day Tokyo was already in place, and some of the roads that led to the castle still exist today. For example, a street called Kagurazaka-dori was constructed along a long slope that led up to the castle's Ushigome Gate, and in the Edo period, many people were overwhelmed by the sight of the magnificent Edo Castle as they climbed it. Today the Kagurazaka district is famous for its fancy stores and restaurants with traditional Edo flavors.

Ushigome Gate

Construction of the castle

Kagurazaka-dori ends at the site of the Outer Moat of Edo Castle. The castle's construction was a great project that involved the entire nation. Many lords were ordered by the Tokugawa government to help complete the castle. Countless huge stones were cut from mountains and shipped by sea. At the bottom of the Kagurazaka slope, you can still see part of these stone walls today.

Past the Outer Moat, there was an area filled with the residences of powerful samurai. Finally, one reached the Inner Moat that surrounded the center of Edo Castle, where the shogun and his government offices could be found.

Omote and Oku

In Edo Castle, the place where samurai bureaucrats worked was called Omote, which means "the front." The place where the shogun spent his private life was called Oku, or "the back." Inside the Oku, there was a place called O-oku, or "the deep back." It was the shogun's harem, where only women could live.

Samurai

The number of samurai directly serving the shogun was almost 15,000. However, if we include their soldiers, the total number of samurai that the shogun could control was more than 80,000.

They worked as bureaucrats to govern Edo and the shogun's property all over Japan. Additionally, there were samurai working for feudal lords. They had offices and houses in Edo, as well as the local domains where their castles were located.

Edo Castle was built as a symbol as well as the practical administrative center for samurai society.

Edo castle and the modern city

Without Edo Castle, Tokyo would not have turned out the way it has today. Merchants and craftspeople flooded to the foot of the castle. They were living in the eastern side of Edo in an area people referred to as Shitamachi, or the Low City. Almost all of this area was created by filling in land during the construction of Edo Castle. The western side gradually expanded, and it was called Yamanote, or the High City. That area was created when local lords and high-ranking samurai constructed their residences and villas.

Edo Castle has been at the center of Shitamachi and Yamanote since Tokugawa Ieyasu founded his government in 1603. Around that time, the salaries of samurai were paid in rice. Therefore, rice was shipped to Edo from all over Japan by boat. There, the merchants

"View of Edo" the right-hand of pair of six-panel folding screens (17th century) Upper right corner is Edo Castle.

converted it to money. These powerful men actually controlled Edo's economy.

Tokyo was built on top of swampland and minor villages around the shore of the bay. When Edo Castle was completed around the middle of the seventeenth century, this city became a lively metropolis that quickly grew to hold a million residents within a hundred years.

It is therefore fair to say that Tokyo is the child of Edo Castle. The city has acquired a priceless cultural inheritance from the people of Edo who lived both inside and outside the castle.

Word List

A

□ **a** 冠 ①1つの, 1人の, ある ②〜につき

□ **able** 形 ①《be - to 〜》（人が）〜することができる ②能力のある

□ **about** 副 ①およそ, 約 ②まわりに, あたりを 前 ①〜について ②〜のまわりに［の］

□ **above** 前 ①〜の上に ②〜より上で, 〜以上で ③〜を超えて 副 ①上に ②以上に 形 上記の 名《the -》上記の人［こと］

□ **above-ground** 形 地上［地表］の［にある・で起きる］

□ **abroad** 副 海外で［に］ **from abroad** 海外から

□ **access** 名 ①接近, 近づく方法, 通路 ②（システムなどへの）アクセス 動 アクセスする

□ **accessible** 形 近づきやすい, 利用できる

□ **accessory** 名 アクセサリー, 服飾品, 装飾品

□ **accommodation** 名 宿泊設備［施設］

□ **according** 副《- to 〜》〜によれば［よると］

□ **achieve** 動 ①〔目的のものを〕獲得する ②〔勝利・名声を〕勝ち取る ③〔努力して目標などを〕成し遂げる

□ **acquire** 動 ①〔時間をかけて努力して〕手に入れる ②〔努力して学力・技術力・知識・習慣などを〕習得する

□ **act** 名 行為, 行い 動 ①行動する ②機能する ③演じる

□ **activity** 名〔ある目的のために人が参加する〕活動, 活発な動作〔動き〕

□ **actor** 名〔演劇・映画などの〕役を演じる人, 役者

□ **actual** 形 実際の, 現実の

□ **actually** 副 実際に, 本当に, 実は

□ **AD** 略〈ラテン語〉紀元後, 西暦〜年（= anno Domini）

□ **add** 動 加える, 付け足す

□ **addition** 名 ①付加, 追加, 添加 ②足し算 **in addition** 加えて, さらに **in addition to** 〜に加えて, さらに

□ **additionally** 副 その上, さらに

□ **address** 名 住所, アドレス

□ **adjacent** 形 隣り合った, 隣接した

□ **administration** 名 管理, 統治, 政権

□ **administrative** 形 ①行政の ②管理の, 運営〔経営〕上の

□ **advance** 名進歩, 前進, 前進 **in advance** 前もって, あらかじめ

□ **adventurous** 形①冒険好きな, 大胆な ②勇気のある, 危険のある

□ **affordable** 形手ごろな[良心的な]価格の

□ **after** 前①〜の後に[で], 〜の次に ②《前後に名詞がきて》次々に〜, 何度も〜《反復・継続を表す》 副後に[で] 接《〜した》後に[で] **after that** その後 動〜の後を追って, 〜を捜して

□ **aftermath** 名（事件などの）余波, 影響

□ **again** 副再び, もう一度

□ **against** 前①〜に対して, 〜に反対して, （規則など）に違反して ②〜にもたれて

□ **agency** 名機関, 政府機関

□ **ago** 副〜前に **long ago** ずっと前に, 昔

□ **agricultural** 形農業の, 農事の

□ **ahead** 副①前方へ[に] ②前もって ③進歩して, 有利に **ahead of 〜** より先[前]に, 〜に先んじて

□ **air** 名①《the −》空中, 空間 ②空気, 《the −》大気 ③雰囲気, 様子 **open air** 戸外, 野外

□ **air-conditioned** 形エアコンのきいた

□ **airport** 名空港

□ **Akasaka** 名赤坂《地名》

□ **Akihabara** 名秋葉原《地名》

□ **alcohol** 名アルコール

□ **alcoholic** 形アルコールの, アルコール性の 名アルコール依存症

□ **all** 形すべての, 〜中 **all kinds of** さまざまな, あらゆる種類の **all over** 〜中で, 全体に亘って, 〜の至る所で **all over the world** 世界中に 代全部, すべて（のもの[人]） 名全体 **first of all** まず第一に 副まったく, すっかり

□ **alley** 名裏通り, 路地, 小道

□ **allied** 動 ally（同盟する）の過去, 過去分詞 形同盟[連合]した, 関連した

□ **allow** 動①許す, 《− … to 〜》…が〜するのを可能にする, …に〜させておく ②与える

□ **almost** 副ほとんど, もう少しで（〜するところ）

□ **alone** 形ただひとりの 副ひとりで, 〜だけで

□ **along** 前〜に沿って 副〜に沿って, 前へ, 進んで **along with 〜** と一緒に **bring along** 持って行く[来る] **walk along** (前へ)歩く, 〜に沿って歩く

□ **alongside** 副そばに, 並んで 前〜のそばに, 〜と並んで

□ **already** 副すでに, もう

□ **also** 副〜も（また）, 〜も同様に 接その上, さらに **not only 〜 but (also) …** 〜だけでなく…もまた

□ **although** 接〜だけれども, 〜にもかかわらず, たとえ〜でも

□ **amazing** 動 amaze（びっくりさせる）の現在分詞 形驚くべき, 見事な

□ **ambiance** 名〔ある場所が醸し出す独特の〕雰囲気, 周囲の環境, ムード

□ **amenity** 名①心地良さ, 快適さ ②生活を便利に[楽しく]するもの[設備・公共施設]

□ **Ameyoko** 名アメ横《「アメヤ横丁」の略。台東区にある地名・商店街名》

□ **among** 前（3つ以上のもの）の間で[に], 〜の中で[に]

□ **amusement** 名娯楽, 楽しみ

□ **an** 冠①1つの, 1人の, ある ②〜につき

□ **ancient** 形昔の, 古代の

□ **and** 接①そして, 〜と… ②《同じ語を結んで》ますます ③《結果を表して》それで, だから

- **anime** 名 日本製アニメーション
- **another** 形 ①もう1つ[1人]の ②別の 代 ①もう1つ[1人] ②別のもの
- **antique** 名 骨董品, アンティーク 形 古風な, 旧式の
- **any** 形 ①《疑問文で》何か, いくつかの ②《否定文で》何も, 少しも(〜ない) ③《肯定文で》どの〜も **any time** いつでも **than any other** ほかのどの〜よりも 代 ①《疑問文で》(〜のうち)何か, どれか, 誰か ②《否定文で》少しも, 何も[誰も]〜ない ③《肯定文で》どれも, 誰でも
- **Aoyama** 名 青山《地名》
- **Aoyama-dori Street** 青山通り《国道246号のうち, 千代田区から渋谷区までの区間の通称》
- **app** 名 アプリ《特に携帯端末やソーシャルメディアなどで使われることが多い》
- **appear** 動 ①現れる, 見えてくる ②(〜のように)見える, 〜らしい
- **appearance** 名 ①現れること, 出現 ②外見, 印象
- **appliance** 名 〔家庭用〕電化製品, 電気器具
- **appoint** 動 〜を任命する, 選任する, 指名する
- **appreciate** 動 ①正しく評価する, よさがわかる ②価値[相場]が上がる ③ありがたく思う
- **approach** 動 ①接近する ②話を持ちかける 名 接近, (〜へ)近づく道
- **approximately** 副 おおよそ, だいたい
- **April** 名 4月
- **Ara-kawa River** 荒川《埼玉県・東京都を流れ東京湾に注ぐ河川》
- **arcade** 名 ①アーケード ②ゲームセンター
- **architect** 名 建築家, 設計者 動 設計する

- **architectural** 形 建築上の
- **are** 動 〜である, (〜に)いる[ある]《主語がyou, we, theyまたは複数名詞のときのbeの現在形》
- **area** 名 ①地域, 地方, 区域, 場所 ②面積
- **around** 副 ①まわりに, あちこちに ②およそ, 約 **get around** あちこちに移動する, 動き回る **go around** 動き回る, あちらこちらに行く **move around** あちこち移動する 前 〜のまわりに, 〜のあちこちに
- **arrangement** 名 ①準備, 手配 ②取り決め, 協定 ③整頓, 配置
- **array** 名 ①配列, 整列 ②大群, 多数
- **arrive** 動 到着する, 到達する **arrive at** 〜に着く
- **art** 名 芸術, 美術 **works of art** 芸術作品
- **artifact** 名 技能(art)によって作り出したもの, 加工品, 工芸品
- **artist** 名 〔芸術作品を作る〕芸術家, アーティスト
- **as** 接 ①《as 〜 as …の形で》…と同じくらい〜 ②〜のとおりに, 〜のように ③〜しながら, 〜しているときに ④〜するにつれて, 〜にしたがって ⑤〜なので ⑥〜だけれども ⑦〜する限りでは 前 ①〜として(の) ②〜の時 副 同じくらい 代 ①〜のような ②〜だが **as a whole** 全体としての **as for** 〜に関しては, 〜はどうかと言うと **as good as** 〜も同然で, ほとんど〜 **as well** なお, その上, 同様に **as well as** 〜と同様に
- **Asakusa** 名 浅草《地名》
- **Asakusa-bashi Bridge** 浅草橋《神田川にかかる橋で, 国道6号(江戸通り)が通る》
- **ash** 名 灰, 燃えがら
- **Asia** 名 アジア
- **Asian** 名 アジア人 形 アジアの
- **ask** 動 ①尋ねる, 聞く ②頼む, 求める

120

□ **aspect** 名①様子, 外見, 姿 ②局面, 側面, 特徴 ③[心に映る]姿, イメージ, 印象

□ **assassinate** 動〔重要人物を〕暗殺する

□ **associate** 動①連合[共同]する, 提携する ②〜を連想する

□ **astonishing** 動 astonish（驚かせる）の現在分詞 形驚くべき

□ **astonishment** 名驚き

□ **at** 前①《場所・時》〜に[で] ②《目標・方向》〜に[を], 〜に向かって ③《原因・理由》〜を見て[聞いて・知って] ④〜に従事して, 〜の状態で **at first** 最初は, 初めのうちは **at that time** その時 **at the end of** 〜の終わりに **at the foot of** 〜のすそ[下部]に **at the time** そのころ, 当時は **at this time** 現時点では, このとき

□ **ate** 動 eat（食べる）の過去

□ **ATM** 名現金自動預け払い機 (= automated/automatic teller machine)

□ **atmosphere** 名①大気, 空気 ②雰囲気

□ **atsukan** 名熱燗, 燗酒《日本酒を加熱したもの》

□ **attention** 名注意, 集中

□ **attract** 動①引き込む, 引き付ける ②魅惑する, 魅了する ③招く, 誘致する

□ **attraction** 名引きつけるもの, 出し物, アトラクション

□ **attractive** 形魅力的な, あいきょうのある

□ **audience** 名聴衆, 視聴者

□ **audio** 形オーディオの, 音の 名オーディオ, 音声部

□ **August** 名8月

□ **author** 名著者, 作家 動著作する, 創作する

□ **autumn** 名秋

□ **available** 形利用[使用・入手]で

きる, 得られる

□ **avenue** 名①並木道 ②《A-, Ave.》〜通り, 〜街

□ **away** 副離れて, 遠くに, 去って, わきに **pass away** 過ぎ去る, 終わる, 死ぬ **walk away** 立ち去る, 遠ざかる 形離れた, 遠征した

□ **Azabu-juban** 名麻布十番《地名》

B

□ **back** 名①背中 ②裏, 後ろ 副①戻って ②後ろへ[に] **step back in time** 少し前の時代に戻る 形裏の, 後ろの 動後ろへ動く, 後退する

□ **bakufu** 名幕府

□ **bamboo** 名竹（類）, 竹材 形竹の

□ **bar** 名酒場

□ **barely** 副①かろうじて, やっと ②ほぼ, もう少しで

□ **base** 名基礎, 土台, 本部 動《 – on 〜》〜に基礎を置く, 基づく

□ **baseball** 名①野球 ②野球用のボール

□ **basement** 名地下（室）, 基部

□ **basic** 形基礎の, 基本の 名《-s》基礎, 基本, 必需品

□ **basin** 名たらい, 洗面器

□ **battle** 名戦闘, 戦い 動戦う

□ **bay** 名湾, 入り江

□ **be** 動〜である, （〜に）いる[ある], 〜となる 助①《現在分詞とともに用いて》〜している ②《過去分詞とともに用いて》〜される, 〜されている

□ **beach** 名海辺, 浜

□ **beautiful** 形美しい, すばらしい 間いいぞ, すばらしい

□ **beauty** 名①美, 美しい人[物] ②《the – 》美点

□ **became** 動 become（なる）の過去

□ **because** 接（なぜなら）〜だから,

～という理由［原因］で **because of** ～のために、～の理由で

□ **become** 動①（～に）なる ②（～に）似合う ③become の過去分詞

□ **bed** 名ベッド、寝床

□ **been** 動 be（～である）の過去分詞 助 be（～している・～される）の過去分詞

□ **beer** 名ビール

□ **before** 前～の前に［で］、～より以前に 接～する前に 副以前に

□ **began** 動 begin（始まる）の過去

□ **begin** 動始まる［始める］、起こる

□ **beginning** 動 begin（始まる）の現在分詞 名初め、始まり

□ **begun** 動 begin（始まる）の過去分詞

□ **behind** 前①～の後ろに、～の背後に ②～に遅れて、～に劣って 副①後ろに、背後に ②遅れて、劣って

□ **being** 動 be（～である）の現在分詞 名存在、生命、人間

□ **believe** 動信じる、信じている、（～と）思う、考える

□ **below** 前①～より下に ②～以下の、～より劣る 副下に［へ］

□ **bento** 名弁当

□ **beside** 前①～のそばに、～と並んで ②～と比べると ③～とはずれて

□ **besides** 前①～に加えて、～のほかに ②〈否定・疑問文で〉～を除いて 副その上、さらに

□ **best** 形最もよい、最大［多］の 副最もよく、最も上手に 名《the－》①最上のもの ②全力、精いっぱい

□ **between** 前（2つのもの）の間に［で・の］ **between A and B** A と B の間に 副間に

□ **beverage** 名飲み物、飲料

□ **beyond** 前～を越えて、～の向こうに 副向こうに

□ **big** 形①大きい ②偉い、重要な

副①大きく、大いに ②自慢して

□ **birth** 名①出産、誕生 ②生まれ、起源、（よい）家柄 **give birth to** ～を生む

□ **bite** 動かむ、かじる 名かむこと、かみ傷、ひと口

□ **black-market** 名闇市

□ **block** 名①（市街地の）1区画 ②大きな固まり、ブロック

□ **bloom** 名①花、開花 ②若さ 動咲く、咲かせる

□ **blossom** 名花 動咲く、開花する

□ **boat** 名ボート、小舟、船 動ボートに乗る［乗せる］、ボートで行く

□ **Bodhisattva Kannon** 観音菩薩（観世音菩薩）

□ **bomb** 動～を爆撃する、～に爆弾を落とす［投下する］

□ **bombing** 名爆撃、爆破

□ **Bonin Islands** ボニン諸島《「小笠原諸島」の別名》

□ **book** 名本、書物

□ **bookshop** 名書店、本屋

□ **bookstore** 名《米》書店

□ **border** 名境界、へり、国境 動①接する、境をなす ②ふちどりをつける

□ **both** 形両方の、2つともの 副《both ～ and … の形で》～も…も両方とも 代両方、両者、双方

□ **bottom** 名①底、下部、すそ野、ふもと、最下位、根底 ②尻 形底の、根底の

□ **bought** 動 buy（買う）の過去、過去分詞

□ **boulevard** 名大通り

□ **boutique** 名〈フランス語〉〔ギフト用品などの〕小規模専門店、〔おしゃれな〕小規模洋品店、ブティック

□ **bowl** 名どんぶり、わん、ボウル

□ **box** 名①箱、容器 ②観覧席 ③詰所

□ **branch** 名①枝 ②支流、支部 動

枝を広げる, 枝分かれする

☐ **brand-name** 形①有名ブランドの ②有名な, 広く知られた

☐ **brick** 名レンガ, レンガ状のもの 形レンガ造りの

☐ **bridge** 名橋 動橋をかける

☐ **bright** 形①輝いている, 鮮明な ②快活な 副輝いて, 明るく

☐ **brightly** 副明るく, 輝いて, 快活に

☐ **bring** 動①持ってくる, 連れてくる ②もたらす, 生じる **bring along** 持って行く[来る]

☐ **British-style** 形イギリス風の

☐ **broad** 形①幅の広い ②寛大な ③明白な 副すっかり, 十分に

☐ **broadcast** 名放送, 番組 動放送する, 広める 形放送の

☐ **broken** 動break（壊す）の過去分詞 形①破れた, 壊れた ②落胆した

☐ **bronze** 名ブロンズ, 青銅

☐ **broth** 名出し汁,（澄んだ）スープ, ブロス

☐ **brought** 動bring（持ってくる）の過去, 過去分詞

☐ **buckwheat** 名①《植物》ソバ（の実） ②そば粉

☐ **buckwheat noodle** そば麺

☐ **Buddhist** 形仏教（徒）の, 仏陀の 名仏教徒

☐ **building** 動build（建てる）の現在分詞 名建物, 建造物, ビルディング

☐ **built** 動build（建てる）の過去, 過去分詞

☐ **bullet** 名銃弾, 弾丸状のもの

☐ **Bunraku** 名文楽

☐ **bureaucrat** 名官僚, 官吏

☐ **burn** 動燃える, 燃焼する

☐ **bus** 名バス

☐ **busily** 副忙しく, せっせと

☐ **business** 名①職業, 仕事 ②商売 ③用事 ④出来事, やっかいなこと 形①職業の ②商売上の

☐ **bustle** 動①忙しく[せかせか]動く ②せき立てる 名せわしげな動き

☐ **bustling** 形〔場所がたくさんの人で〕にぎわっている, 活気のある

☐ **busy** 形忙しい

☐ **but** 接①でも, しかし ②〜を除いて **not only 〜 but（also）…** 〜だけでなく…もまた 副〜を除いて, 〜のほかは 副ただ, のみ, ほんの

☐ **buy** 動買う, 獲得する 名購入, 買った[買える]物

☐ **by** 前①《位置》〜のそばに[で] ②《手段・方法・行為者・基準》〜によって, 〜で ③《期限》〜までには ④《通過・経由》〜を経由して, 〜を通って 副そばに, 通り過ぎて **by far** はるかに, 断然

C

☐ **call** 動①呼ぶ, 叫ぶ ②電話をかける ③立ち寄る 名①呼び声, 叫び ②電話（をかけること） ③短い訪問

☐ **can** 助①〜できる ②〜してもよい ③〜でありうる ④《否定文で》〜のはずがない 名缶, 容器 動缶詰[瓶詰]にする

☐ **canal** 名運河, 用水路

☐ **capacity** 名①定員, 容量 ②能力,（潜在的な）可能性

☐ **capital** 名首都 形首都の

☐ **capsule** 名カプセル 形小型の

☐ **capture** 動捕える 名捕えること, 捕獲（物）

☐ **car** 名自動車,（列車の）車両

☐ **card** 名カード, 券, 名刺, はがき

☐ **care** 名①心配, 注意 ②世話, 介護 **take care of** 〜の世話をする, 〜面倒を見る 動①《通例否定文・疑問文で》気にする, 心配する ②世話をする

□ **careful** 形注意深い, 慎重な

□ **carry** 動①運ぶ, 連れていく, 持ち歩く ②伝わる, 伝える

□ **case** 名①事件, 問題, 事柄 ②実例, 場合 ③実状, 状況, 症状 ④箱 **in case of** 〜の場合には

□ **castle** 名城, 大邸宅

□ **casual** 形①偶然の ②略式の, カジュアルな ③おざなりの

□ **cater** 動①料理を提供する[賄う] ②〔要求などに〕応じる, 迎合する

□ **celebrate** 動①祝う, 祝福する ②祝典を開く

□ **cemetery** 名共同墓地

□ **center** 名①中心, 中央 ②中心地 [人物] 動集中する[させる]

□ **central** 形中央の, 主要な

□ **centralized** 形中央集権化の

□ **century** 名100年間, 1世紀

□ **certain** 形①確実な, 必ず〜する ②(人が)確信した ③ある ④いくらかの 代(〜の中の)いくつか

□ **chain** 名①鎖 ②一続き

□ **chair** 名いす

□ **chance** 名①偶然, 運 ②好機, 見込み 形偶然の, 思いがけない 動偶然見つける

□ **change** 動①変わる, 変える ②交換する ③両替する 名①変化, 変更 ②取り替え, 乗り換え ③つり銭, 小銭

□ **chaos** 名無秩序, 混乱状態

□ **chaotic** 形大混乱の, 雑然とした, 混沌とした

□ **chapter** 名(書物の)章

□ **character** 名①特性, 個性 ②(小説・劇などの)登場人物 ③文字, 記号 ④品性, 人格

□ **characteristic** 名特徴, 特色, 持ち味

□ **charge** 名請求金額, 料金

□ **charming** 動 charm (魅了する)の現在分詞 形魅力的な, チャーミングな

□ **cheaply** 副安く, 安っぽく

□ **chef** 名シェフ, 料理長

□ **cherish** 動①大切にする, (思い出などを)胸にしまっておく ②(アイデアなどを)温める ③(希望・イメージなどを)抱く

□ **cherry** 名サクランボ, 桜

□ **Chiba Prefecture** 千葉県

□ **chicken** 名①ニワトリ(鶏) ②鶏肉, チキン 形臆病な

□ **chief** 名頭, 長, 親分 形最高位の, 第一の, 主要な

□ **child** 名子ども

□ **Chinese** 形中国(人)の 名①中国人 ②中国語

□ **choose** 動選ぶ, (〜に)決める

□ **chosen** 動 choose (選ぶ)の過去分詞 **be chosen as** 〜として選ばれる 形選ばれた, 精選された

□ **Chuo and Sobu Lines** 中央・総武線《千葉県にある千葉駅から, 東京都の御茶ノ水駅を経由して三鷹駅までを各駅停車で結ぶ, JR東日本の運転系統の通称》

□ **Chuo-dori** 名中央通り《港区から中央区を経由し, 台東区に至る道路の通称》

□ **circle** 名①円, 円周, 輪 ②循環, 軌道

□ **citizen** 名①市民, 国民 ②住民, 民間人

□ **city** 名①都市, 都会 ②《the ‒》(全)市民

□ **city hall** 市庁舎, 市役所

□ **civil** 形①一般人の, 民間(人)の ②国内の, 国家の ③礼儀正しい

□ **civil war** 内戦, 内乱

□ **civilization** 名文明, 文明人(化)

□ **clan** 名①氏族 ②一家, 一門

□ **class** 名①学級, 組, 階級 ②授業

動 分類する，等級をつける

- [ ] **classical** 形 古典的の，クラシックの
- [ ] **clean** 形 ①きれいな，清潔な ②正当な
- [ ] **climate** 名 気候，風土，環境
- [ ] **climb** 動 登る，徐々に上がる 名 登ること，上昇
- [ ] **close** 形 ①近い ②親しい ③狭い 副 ①接近して ②密集して 動 ①閉まる，閉める ②終える，閉店する
- [ ] **closed** 動 close（閉まる）の過去，過去分詞 形 閉じた，閉鎖した
- [ ] **closely** 副 ①密接に ②念入りに，詳しく ③ぴったりと
- [ ] **clothing** 名 衣類，衣料品
- [ ] **club** 名 クラブ，（同好）会
- [ ] **coast** 名 海岸，沿岸
- [ ] **coffee** 名 コーヒー
- [ ] **coin** 名 硬貨，コイン 動（硬貨を）鋳造する
- [ ] **cold** 形 ①寒い，冷たい ②冷淡な，冷静な 名 ①寒さ，冷たさ ②風邪
- [ ] **collection** 名 収集，収蔵物
- [ ] **color** 名 ①色，色彩 ②絵の具 ③血色 動 色をつける
- [ ] **color-coded** 形〔識別しやすくするために〕色分けされた
- [ ] **combined** 形 ①結び付いた ②複合の，共同の ③一体化した，統合された
- [ ] **come** 動 ①来る，行く，現れる ②（出来事が）起こる，生じる ③～になる ④comeの過去形
- [ ] **comfortable** 形 快適な，心地いい
- [ ] **comfortably** 副 心地よく，くつろいで
- [ ] **coming** 動 come（来る）の現在分詞 形 今度の，来たるべき 名 到来，来ること
- [ ] **commercial** 形 商業の，営利的な 名 コマーシャル
- [ ] **commodity** 名 ①〔サービスと対

比される〕商品，売買品 ②〔ブランド品と対比される〕日用品，生活必需品

- [ ] **commodore** 名 海軍准将，提督
- [ ] **Commodore Perry** ペリー提督《マシュー・カルブレイス・ペリー（Matthew Calbraith Perry）アメリカ海軍の軍人，1794–1858》
- [ ] **common** 形 ①共通の，共同の ②普通の，平凡な ③一般の，公共の 名 ①共有地 ②公園
- [ ] **commonly** 副 一般に，通例
- [ ] **communication** 名 ①〔情報の〕やりとり，連絡，伝達 ②〔お互いの〕意思疎通，共感 ③〔手紙や電話などの〕通信手段
- [ ] **commute** 動 通勤する，通学する 名 通学，通勤
- [ ] **commuter** 形 通勤（通学）の
- [ ] **company** 名 会社
- [ ] **compare** 動 ①比較する，対照する ②たとえる
- [ ] **compassionate** 形 思いやりのある，慈悲深い，心の優しい
- [ ] **complement** 動 ①～を補完する，引き立たせる ②《料理》ぴったり合わせる，よく合わせる
- [ ] **complete** 形 完全な，まったくの，完成した 動 完成させる
- [ ] **complex** 形 入り組んだ，複雑な，複合の 名 複合体，複合施設
- [ ] **complicated** 動 complicate（複雑にする）の過去，過去分詞 形 ①複雑な ②むずかしい，困難な
- [ ] **concentrated** 動 concentrate（一点に集める）の過去，過去分詞 形 ①集中した ②凝縮された，高濃度の，濃厚な
- [ ] **concentration** 名 ①集中，集中力，集合 ②濃縮，濃度
- [ ] **concert** 名 音楽会，演奏会，コンサート
- [ ] **Confucianism** 名 儒教
- [ ] **confused** 動 confuse（混同する）

の過去, 過去分詞 形困惑した, 混乱した

□ **confusing** 形混乱させる, 紛らわしい

□ **connect** 動つながる, つなぐ, 関係づける

□ **consider** 動～と考える[見なす・認める]

□ **consistency** 名①一貫性 ②粘り, 濃度

□ **consolidate** 動①～を強固にする, 確固たるものとする ②～を統一する, 集約する, 確立する

□ **constant** 形①絶えない, 一定の, 不変の ②不屈の, 確固たる 名定数

□ **construct** 動組み立てる, 建設する, 建造する

□ **construction** 名構造, 建設, 工事, 建物

□ **contain** 動①含む, 入っている ②(感情などを)抑える

□ **content** 名《-s》中身, 内容, 目次 ②満足 形満足して 動満足する[させる]

□ **continue** 動続く, 続ける, (中断後)再開する, (ある方向に)移動していく

□ **contrast** 名対照, 対比 動対照させる, よい対象となる

□ **control** 動①管理[支配]する ②抑制する, コントロールする 名①管理, 支配(力) ②抑制

□ **controversial** 形論争上の, 議論の余地のある

□ **convenience** 名便利(さ), 便利なもの, 利便性

□ **convenient** 形便利な, 好都合な

□ **conveniently** 副好都合に, 便利に

□ **convention** 名①慣習, しきたり ②会議, 集会, 大会 ③協定

□ **conversation** 名会話, 会談

□ **convert** 動①〔～の性質や形を〕変える ②〔財産などを等価のものに〕換金[交換]する

□ **conveyor-belt** 名ベルト・コンベヤー

□ **cook** 動料理する, (食物が)煮える 名料理人, コック

□ **cooking** 動cook(料理する)の過去, 過去分詞 名料理(法), クッキング

□ **core** 名核心, 中心, 芯

□ **corner** 名①曲がり角, 角 ②すみ, はずれ

□ **correct** 形正しい, 適切な, りっぱな 動(誤りを)訂正する, 直す

□ **cosmopolitan** 名コスモポリタン, 世界主義者, 国際人 形国際的な, (立場にとらわれない)世界主義的な

□ **cosplay** 名コスプレ《日本語より。もともとは「コスチューム・プレイ」》

□ **cotton** 名①綿, 綿花 ②綿織物, 綿糸

□ **could** 助①can(～できる)の過去 ②《控え目な推量・可能性・願望などを表す》

□ **count** 動①数える ②(～を…と)みなす ③重要[大切]である count ～ as… (～を…と)みなす 名計算, 総計, 勘定

□ **counter** 名(店の)売り台, カウンター, 計算器

□ **countless** 形無数の, 数え切れない

□ **country** 名①国 ②《the－》田舎, 郊外 ③地域, 領域, 分野 形田舎の, 野暮な

□ **couple** 名①2つ, 対 ②夫婦, 一組 ③数個 動つなぐ, つながる, 関連させる

□ **course** 名①進路, 方向 ②経過, 成り行き ③科目, 講座 ④策, 方策 of course もちろん, 当然

□ **court** 名①中庭, コート ②法廷, 裁判所 ③宮廷, 宮殿

- ☐ **courteous** 形礼儀正しい, ていねいな

- ☐ **cove** 名①入り江, 小さな湾 ②〔山の〕小さな谷間, 洞窟 ③〔丘や森の〕細い道

- ☐ **coworker** 名〔職場の〕同僚

- ☐ **craftsmen** 名craftsman（職人）の複数

- ☐ **craftspeople** 名〔熟練した〕職人たち, 工匠たち《craftspersonの複数形》

- ☐ **cram** 動〔人や物を無理に〕詰め込む, 押し込む

- ☐ **create** 動創造する, 生み出す, 引き起こす

- ☐ **creative** 形創造力のある, 独創的な

- ☐ **creator** 名創作者, 創造者, 神

- ☐ **credit** 名①信用, 評判, 名声 ②掛け売り, 信用貸し 動信用する

- ☐ **crime** 名①（法律上の）罪, 犯罪 ②悪事, よくない行為

- ☐ **criminal** 形犯罪の, 罪深い, 恥ずべき 名犯罪者, 犯人

- ☐ **crisscross** 動縦横に動かす, 交差させる

- ☐ **cross** 動①横切る, 渡る ②じゃまする ③十字を切る

- ☐ **crossing** 動cross（横切る）の過去, 過去分詞 名横断, 交差点, 横断歩道, 踏み切り

- ☐ **crowd** 動群がる, 混雑する 名群集, 雑踏, 多数, 聴衆

- ☐ **crowded** 動crowd（群がる）の過去, 過去分詞 形混雑した, 満員の

- ☐ **cruise** 名〔船旅の〕クルージング

- ☐ **cuisine** 名料理, 料理法

- ☐ **culinary** 形料理の, 台所の

- ☐ **cultural** 形文化の, 文化的な

- ☐ **culture** 名①文化 ②教養 ③耕作, 栽培 動耕す, 栽培する

- ☐ **cultured** 形文化のある, 教養のある

- ☐ **current** 形現在の, 目下の, 通用[流通]している 名流れ, 電流, 風潮

- ☐ **currently** 副今のところ, 現在

- ☐ **custom** 名①習慣, 慣例, 風俗 ②顧客, ひいき, 得意先 ③《-s》関税,《the -s》税関 形注文の

- ☐ **customer** 名顧客

- ☐ **cut** 動①切る, 刈る ②短縮する, 削る ③cutの過去, 過去分詞

D

- ☐ **Daikan-yama** 名代官山《地名》

- ☐ **daily** 形毎日の, 日常の 副毎日, 日ごとに

- ☐ **daimyo** 名大名

- ☐ **date** 名①日付, 年月日 ②デート 動①日付を記す ②デートする

- ☐ **day** 名①日中, 昼間 ②日, 期日 ③《-s》時代, 生涯 **each day** 毎日, 日ごとに **every day** 毎日 **these days** このごろ

- ☐ **Dazaifu** 名太宰府（市）《福岡県の中西部, 筑紫地域に位置する市。太宰府天満宮や多くの史跡がある》

- ☐ **decide** 動decide（決定する）の過去, 過去分詞 **decide to do** ～することに決める 形はっきりした, 断固とした

- ☐ **deck** 名（船の）デッキ, 甲板, 階, 床

- ☐ **decline** 動①断る ②傾く ③衰える 名①傾くこと ②下り坂, 衰え, 衰退

- ☐ **décor** 名室内装飾, 装飾様式

- ☐ **decoration** 名飾り付け, 装飾

- ☐ **deep** 形①深い, 深さ～の ②深遠な ③濃い 副深く

- ☐ **defense** 名①防御, 守備 ②国防 ③弁護, 弁明

- ☐ **delicacy** 名ごちそう, 美味, 珍味

127

□ **delicious** 形おいしい, うまい

□ **delight** 動喜ぶ, 喜ばす, 楽しむ, 楽しませる 名喜び, 愉快

□ **demand** 動①要求する, 尋ねる ②必要とする 名①要求, 請求 ②需要

□ **densely** 副密集して

□ **depa-chika** 名デパ地下《日本の百貨店 (デパート) の地下階にある食料品売り場を指す通称》

□ **depart** 動①出発する ②(常道などから) はずれる

□ **department** 名①部門, 課, 局, 担当分野 ②《D-》《米国・英国の)省

□ **depend** 動《– on [upon] ~》①~を頼る, ~をあてにする ②~による

□ **depict** 動 [絵・映像・文章・発話などで] ~を描写する [表現する]

□ **design** 動~を設計する, デザインする

□ **destination** 名行き先, 目的地

□ **destroy** 動破壊する, 絶滅させる, 無効にする

□ **destruction** 名破壊 (行為・状態)

□ **detached** 動 detach (引き離す) の過去, 過去分詞 形引き離された, 離れた

□ **determined** 動 determine (決心する) の過去, 過去分詞 形決心した, 決然とした

□ **develop** 動①発達する [させる] ②開発する

□ **developing** 動 develop (発達する) の現在分詞 形発展 [開発] 途上の

□ **development** 名①発達, 発展 ②開発

□ **devoted** 動 devote (捧げる) の過去, 過去分詞 形献身的な, 熱心な, 愛情深い

□ **dictator** 名独裁者, 専制者

□ **did** 動 do (~をする) の過去 助 do の過去

□ **different** 形異なった, 違った, 別の, さまざま

□ **dining** 動 dine (食事をする) の現在分詞 名食事, 夕食をとること

□ **dinner** 名①ディナー, 夕食 ②夕食 [食事] 会, 祝宴

□ **direction** 名①方向, 方角 ②《-s》指示, 説明書 ③指導, 指揮 **in the direction of** ~の方向に

□ **directly** 副①じかに ②まっすぐに ③ちょうど

□ **disappear** 動見えなくなる, 姿を消す, なくなる

□ **disaster** 名①[突然起こる大規模な] 災害, 天災 ②思いがけない大きな不幸, 大惨事

□ **discover** 動発見する, 気づく

□ **dish** 名①大皿 ②料理

□ **display** 動展示する, 示す 名展示, 陳列, 表出

□ **distance** 名距離, 隔たり, 遠方

□ **distilled** 形蒸留された

□ **distinctive** 形独特の, 特色 [特徴] のある

□ **district** 名①地方, 地域 ②行政区

□ **diverse** 形①種々の, 多様な ②異なった

□ **do** 助 do ①《ほかの動詞とともに用いて現在形の否定文・疑問文をつくる》②《同じ動詞を繰り返す代わりに用いる》③《動詞を強調するのに用いる》動~をする

□ **does** 動 do (~をする) の3人称単数現在 助 do の3人称単数現在

□ **dog** 名犬

□ **doll** 名人形

□ **domain** 名①統治地域, 領土 ②領域, 分野

□ **dome** 名丸屋根, ドーム

□ **domestic** 形①家庭の ②国内の, 自国の, 国産の

□ **donate** 動寄付する, 寄贈する

- **door** 名①ドア, 戸 ②一軒, 一戸
- **dormitory** 名寄宿舎, 寮
- **double-arched** 形二重アーチの
- **download** 動〜をダウンロードする
- **downtown** 副商業地区［繁華街］へ 形商業地区［繁華街］の 名街の中心, 繁華街
- **dozen** 名1ダース, 12（個）
- **drink** 動飲む, 飲酒する 名飲み物, 酒, 1杯
- **drinking** 動drink（飲む）の現在分詞 名飲むこと, 飲酒
- **due** 形予定された, 期日のきている, 支払われるべき **due to** 〜によって, 〜が原因で 名当然の権利
- **dug** 動dig（掘る）の過去, 過去分詞
- **during** 前〜の間（ずっと）
- **dynamic** 形活動的な, 動的な, ダイナミックな
- **dynamism** 名力強さ, ダイナミズム

E

- **each** 形それぞれの, 各自の 代それぞれ, 各自 副それぞれに **each day** 毎日, 日ごとに **each other** お互いに
- **early** 形①（時間や時期が）早い ②初期の, 幼少の, 若い 副①早く, 早めに ②初期に, 初めのころに
- **earthquake** 名地震, 大変動
- **easily** 副①容易に, たやすく, 苦もなく ②気楽に
- **east** 名《the 〜》東, 東部, 東方 形東の, 東方［東部］
- **East Japan Railway** 東日本旅客鉄道（JR東日本）
- **eastern** 形①東方の, 東向きの ②東洋の, 東洋風の

- **easy** 形①やさしい, 簡単な ②気楽な, くつろいだ
- **eat** 動食べる, 食事する
- **Ebisu** 名恵比寿《地名》
- **economic** 形経済学の, 経済上の
- **economy** 名①経済, 財政 ②節約
- **edge** 名①刃 ②端, 縁
- **Edo** 名江戸《東京の旧称》
- **Edo Bay** 江戸湾《近世（およそ江戸後期）の東京湾を指す, 明治時代以降の造語》
- **Edo Castle** 江戸城
- **Edo clan** 江戸氏《武蔵国を発祥とする中世の武家》
- **Edo-based** 形江戸を拠点とする
- **Edo-gawa River** 江戸川《関東地方を流れる利根川水系の河川》
- **Edo-period** 名江戸時代《1603–1868》
- **Edo-Tokyo Museum** 江戸東京博物館《墨田区にある都立の博物館。江戸・東京の歴史・文化に関わる資料を収集, 保存, 展示している》
- **Edo-Tokyo Open Air Architectural Museum** 江戸東京たてもの園《小金井市にある野外博物館で, 江戸東京博物館の分館。江戸・東京の歴史的な建物を移築保存し展示している》
- **Edogawa** 名江戸川（区）《地名》
- **edomae** 名江戸前《「江戸風」の意。もとは「江戸の前の海」の意で, 江戸湾でとれる新鮮な魚類も指す》
- **efficient** 形①効率的な, 有効な ②有能な, 敏腕な
- **Eiffel Tower** 《the 〜》エッフェル塔
- **eight** 名8（の数字）, 8人［個］ 形8の, 8人［個］の
- **eighteenth** 名第18番目（の人［もの］）, 18日 形第18番目の
- **either** 形①（2つのうち）どちらかの ②どちらでも 代どちらも, どち

らでも 副 ①どちらか ②《否定文で》
～もまた(…ない) 接《-～or…》～
かまたは…か

□ **elderly** 形かなり年配の, 初老の
名《the－》お年寄り

□ **electronic** 形電子工学の, エレク
トロニクスの

□ **electronics** 名エレクトロニクス,
電子工学, 電子機器

□ **elegant** 形上品な, 優雅な

□ **elevated** 動elevate (上げる) の過
去, 過去分詞 形①高い, 高潔な ②高
くなった

□ **eleventh** 名第11番目 (の人[物]),
11日 形第11番目の

□ **elite** 名エリート, えり抜き 形エリ
ートの, 一流の, えり抜きの

□ **embankment** 名土手, (護岸) 堤
防, 盛り土

□ **embassy** 名大使館

□ **embody** 動具体化する, 具体的に
表現する

□ **emerge** 動表面に出てくる, 出現
する

□ **emergency** 名非常時, 緊急時
形緊急の

□ **emperor** 名皇帝, 天皇

□ **Emperor Meiji** 明治天皇《日
本の第122代天皇。1852–1912 (在位
1867–1912)》

□ **employee** 名従業員, 会社員

□ **Empress Meiji** 名明治天皇の皇
后《昭憲皇太后。1849–1914》

□ **encounter** 動〔偶然・思いがけな
く〕出会う, 出くわす

□ **end** 名①終わり, 終末, 死 ②果て,
末, 端 ③目的 at the end of ～の終
わりに 動終わる, 終える

□ **English** 名①英語 ②《the－》英
国人 形①英語の ②英国 (人) の

□ **enjoy** 動楽しむ, 享受する enjoy
doing ～するのを楽しむ

□ **enjoyable** 形楽しめる, 愉快な

□ **enlightened** 形①正しい知識[情
報]を持った, 見識ある ②啓発[啓蒙]
された ③悟りに達した

□ **enlightenment** 名啓発, 啓蒙,
教化

□ **enormous** 形ばく大な, 非常に大
きい, 巨大な

□ **enough** 形十分な, (～するに) 足
る 代十分 (な量・数), たくさん 副 (～
できる) だけ, 十分に, まったく

□ **enrich** 動①〔人や国などを〕裕福
[金持ち]にする ②〔～の質や価値な
どを〕高める

□ **enshrine** 動〔神聖なものとして〕
祭る, 安置する

□ **enter** 動①入る, 入会[入学]する
[させる] ②記入する ③ (考えなど
が) (心・頭に) 浮かぶ

□ **entertaining** 形面白い, 愉快な,
楽しませる

□ **entertainment** 名①楽しみ, 娯
楽 ②もてなし, 歓待

□ **enthusiastic** 形熱狂的な, 熱烈
な

□ **entire** 形全体の, 完全な, まったく
の

□ **entrance** 名①入り口, 入場 ②開
始

□ **environment** 名①環境 ②周囲
(の状況), 情勢

□ **equivalent** 形①同等の, 等しい
②同意義の 名同等のもの, 等価なも
の

□ **era** 名時代, 年代

□ **especially** 副特別に, とりわけ

□ **essence** 名①本質, 真髄, 最重要
点 ②エッセンス, エキス

□ **essential** 形本質的な, 必須の 名
本質, 要点, 必需品

□ **establish** 動〔会社や学校などの
組織を〕設置[設立・創設・創業]する

□ **estate** 名地所, 私有地

□ **Europe** 名ヨーロッパ

□ **even** 副①《強意》〜でさえも、〜ですら、いっそう、なおさら ②平等に **even if** たとえ〜でも **even though** 〜であるけれども、〜にもかかわらず 形①平らな、水平の ②等しい、均一の ③落ち着いた 動平らになる[する]、釣り合いがとれる

□ **evening** 名夕方、晩

□ **event** 名出来事、事件、イベント

□ **eventually** 副結局は

□ **ever** 副①今までに、これまで、かつて、いつまでも ②《強意》いったい

□ **every** 形①どの〜も、すべての、あらゆる ②毎〜、〜ごとの **every day** 毎日

□ **everyday** 形毎日の、日々の

□ **everything** 代すべてのこと[もの]、何でも、何もかも

□ **everywhere** 副どこにいても、いたるところに

□ **evolve** 動〔徐々に〕〜を発達[発展・展開]させる

□ **example** 名例、見本、模範 **for example** たとえば

□ **excellent** 形優れた、優秀な

□ **exclusive** 形排他的な、独占的な

□ **exhibit** 動〔作品などを公然と〕展示する、発表する

□ **exist** 動存在する、生存する、ある、いる

□ **existence** 名存在、実在、生存

□ **exit** 名出口、退去 動退出する、退去する

□ **expand** 動〔大きさ・数量・程度などを〕大きくする、拡大する

□ **expensive** 形高価な、ぜいたくな

□ **experience** 名経験、体験 動経験[体験]する

□ **exploration** 名探検、実地調査

□ **explore** 動探検[調査]する、切り開く

□ **export** 動〜を輸出する、運び去る

□ **express** 名速達便、急行列車

□ **extensive** 形広い、広範囲に渡る、大規模な

□ **extremely** 副非常に、極度に

F

□ **fabulous** 形すばらしい、すてきな、途方もない

□ **face** 名①顔、顔つき ②外観、外見 ③(時計の)文字盤、(建物の)正面 動直面する、立ち向かう

□ **facility** 名①《-ties》施設、設備 ②器用さ、容易さ

□ **fair** 形①正しい、公平[正当]な ②快晴の ③色白の、金髪の ④かなりの ⑤《古》美しい 副①公平に、きれいに ②見事に

□ **fairly** 副①公平に ②かなり、相当に

□ **faithful** 形忠実な、正確な

□ **fall** 動①落ちる、倒れる ②(値段・温度が)下がる ③(ある状態に)急に陥る 名①落下、墜落 ②滝 ③崩壊 ④秋

□ **family** 名家族、家庭、一門、家柄

□ **famous** 形有名な、名高い **be famous for** 〜で有名である

□ **fan** 名①愛好者 ②扇(状のもの)、うちわ

□ **fancy** 形①装飾的な、見事な ②法外な、高級な

□ **fantastic** 形空想的な、奇想天外な、風変わりな、すばらしい

□ **far** 副①遠くに、はるかに、離れて ②《比較級を強めて》ずっと、はるかに **by far** はるかに、断然 **far from** 〜から遠い 形遠い、向こうの 名遠方

□ **fare** 名運賃、料金

□ **fare-adjustment machine**

131

乗車賃金精算機, のりこし精算機

□ **farther** 副もっと遠く, さらに先に 形もっと向こうの, さらに進んだ

□ **fascinating** 動fascinate (魅惑する)の現在分詞 形魅惑的な, うっとりさせるような

□ **fashion** 名①流行, 方法, はやり ②流行のもの(特に服装)

□ **fashionable** 形①流行の ②上流社会の

□ **fast-paced** 形ペースの速い, 急速な

□ **favorite** 名お気に入り(の人[物]) 形お気に入りの, ひいきの

□ **feature** 動①(～の)特徴になる ②呼び物にする

□ **feel** 動感じる, (～と)思う **feel like** ～のような感じがする

□ **ferry** 名渡し場, フェリーボート 動船で渡す, フェリーで川を渡る

□ **feudal** 形封建制度の, 封建的な

□ **feudal domain** 封建領地, 藩

□ **feudal lord** 〔中世の〕(封建)領主, 大名

□ **few** 形①ほとんどない, 少数の(～しかない) ②《a－》少数の, 少しはある 代少数の人[物]

□ **fifteenth** 名第15番目(の人[物]), 15日 形第15番目の

□ **fifty** 名50(の数字), 50人[個] 形50の, 50人[個]の

□ **figure** 名①人[物]の姿, 形 ②図(形) ③人物, 大人物, 大立者

□ **fill** 動①満ちる, 満たす ②《be -ed with ～》～でいっぱいである

□ **film** 名①フィルム, 映画 ②膜 動映画を製作[撮影]する

□ **final** 形最後の, 決定的な 名最後のもの

□ **finally** 副最後に, ついに, 結局

□ **financial** 形①財務(上)の, 金融(上)の ②金融関係者の

□ **find** 動①見つける ②(～と)わかる, 気づく, ～と考える ③得る

□ **fire** 名①火, 炎, 火事 ②砲火, 攻撃

□ **Fire Museum** 消防博物館《新宿区の四谷消防署に併設されており, 東京消防庁の歴史と活動に関する資料を展示している》

□ **firefighting** 名消火活動, 消防

□ **firm** 名会社, 事務所

□ **first** 名最初, 第一(の人・物) **at first** 最初は, 初めのうちは **first of all** まず第一に 形①第一の, 最初の ②最も重要な 副第一に, 最初に

□ **fish** 名魚 動釣りをする

□ **fishermen** 名漁師《fishermanの複数形》

□ **five** 名5(の数字), 5人[個] 形5の, 5人[個]の

□ **flat** 形①平らな ②しぼんだ, 空気の抜けた 副①平らに, 平たく ②きっかり

□ **flat-bottomed** 形平底の

□ **flavor** 名風味, 味わい, 趣 動風味を添える

□ **flexibility** 名①〔変化に対する〕適応性, 順応性 ②〔人の〕従順さ, 素直さ

□ **flight** 名飛ぶこと, 飛行, (飛行機の)フライト

□ **flood** 名①洪水 ②殺到 動①氾濫する, 氾濫させる ②殺到する

□ **floor** 名床, 階

□ **flow** 動流れ出る, 流れる, あふれる 名①流出 ②流ちょう(なこと)

□ **folk-craft** 名民芸

□ **folksy** 形気取らない, 庶民的な

□ **follow** 動ついていく, あとをたどる

□ **follower** 名後続する者, 後継者

□ **food** 名食物, えさ, 肥料

□ **food-related** 形食(品)関連の

□ **foodstuff** 名食料(品), 食材, 食品

132

□ **foot** 名①足, 足取り ②(山などの)ふもと, (物の)最下部, すそ **at the foot of** 〜のすそ[下部]に **on foot** 歩いて

□ **football** 名(英国で)サッカー, (米国で)アメリカンフットボール

□ **for** 前①《目的・原因・対象》〜にとって, 〜のために[の], 〜に対して ②《期間》〜間 ③《代理》〜の代わりに ④《方向》〜へ(向かって) **as for** 〜に関しては, 〜はどうかと言うと **for example** たとえば **for instance** たとえば **for 〜 years** 〜年間, 〜年にわたって **It is 〜 for someone to** … (人)が…するのは〜だ 接 というわけは〜, なぜなら〜, だから

□ **foreign** 形外国の, よその, 異質な

□ **foreigner** 名①外国人 ②〈話〉よそ者

□ **forest** 名森林

□ **forget** 動忘れる, 置き忘れる **forget to do** 〜することを忘れる

□ **form** 名①形, 形式 ②書式 動形づくる

□ **former** 形①前の, 先の, 以前の ②《the –》(二者のうち)前者の

□ **forth** 副前へ, 外へ

□ **fortress** 名要塞, 堅固な場所

□ **fortune** 名①富, 財産 ②幸運, 繁栄, チャンス ③運命, 運勢

□ **found** 動①find (見つける)の過去, 過去分詞 ②〜の基礎を築く, 〜を設立する

□ **foundation** 名①建設, 創設 ②基礎, 土台

□ **four** 名4(の数字), 4人[個] 形4の, 4人[個]の

□ **free** 形①自由な, 開放された, 自由に〜できる ②暇で, (物が)空いている, 使える ③無料の 副①自由に ②無料で 動自由にする, 解放する

□ **free-standing** 形自立型の, 独立の

□ **French** 形フランス(人・語)の

名①フランス語 ②《the –》フランス人

□ **frequent** 形ひんぱんな, よくある 動よく訪れる, 交際する

□ **fresh** 形①新鮮な, 生気のある ②さわやかな, 清純な ③新規の

□ **fried** 動fry (油で揚げる)の過去, 過去分詞 形油で揚げた, フライ料理の

□ **friend** 名友だち, 仲間

□ **from** 前①《出身・出発点・時間・順序・原料》〜から ②《原因・理由》〜がもとで **far from** 〜から遠い **from abroad** 海外から **from one side to the other** 一方の側から他の側へ **from 〜 to** … 〜から…まで

□ **front** 名正面, 前 **in front of** 〜の前に, 〜の正面に 形正面の, 前面の

□ **fruit** 名①果実, 実 ②《-s》成果, 利益 動実を結ぶ

□ **Fukagawa** 名深川《地名》

□ **Fukagawa Edo Museum** 深川江戸資料館《江東区立の資料館。江戸時代に関する資料等を収集, 保存及び展示している》

□ **Fukuoka** 名福岡(県・市)《地名》

□ **Fukutoshin** 名副都心《大都市において, 都市内域と郊外の交通接点を中心として発達し, 都心の機能を代替する地域》

□ **full** 形①満ちた, いっぱいの, 満期の ②完全な, 盛りの, 充実した **be full of** 〜で一杯である 名全部

G

□ **gain** 動①得る, 増す ②進歩する, 進む 名①増加, 進歩 ②利益, 得ること, 獲得

□ **game** 名ゲーム, 試合, 遊び, 競技 動賭けごとをする

□ **garden** 名庭, 庭園 動園芸をする, 庭いじりをする

□ **gas** 名①ガス, 気体 ②ガソリン

A
B
C
D
E
F
G
H
I
J
K
L
M
N
O
P
Q
R
S
T
U
V
W
X
Y
Z

動 ガス［ガソリン］を供給する

- □ **gate** 名 ①門, 扉, 入り口 ②（空港・駅などの）ゲート

- □ **gateway** 名 出入り口, 道

- □ **gather** 動 ①集まる, 集める ②生じる, 増す ③推測する

- □ **Gauguin** 《Paul –》ゴーガン（ポール・ゴーギャン）《フランスのポスト印象派の画家。1848–1903》

- □ **gave** 動 give（与える）の過去

- □ **GDP** 略 国内総生産（= gross domestic product）

- □ **gear** 動 ～の調子を合わせる, ～を適合させる

- □ **general** 形 ①全体の, 一般の, 普通の ②おおよその ③（職位の）高い, 上級の 名 大将, 将軍

- □ **generally** 副 ①一般に, だいたい ②たいてい

- □ **generate** 動 ～を生む, ～を起こす

- □ **genre** 名 〔芸術の〕分野, ジャンル, 部門

- □ **geography** 名 地理, 地理学

- □ **get** 動 ①得る, 手に入れる ②（ある状態に）なる, いたる ③わかる, 理解する ④～させる, する ⑤（…の状態に）する ⑤（ある場所に）達する, 着く **get around** あちこちに移動する, 動き回る **get off** （～から）降りる **get on**（電車などに）乗る **get there** そこに到達する **get to** ～に達する［到達する・到着する］

- □ **Ghibli Museum** （三鷹の森）ジブリ美術館《三鷹市立のアニメーション美術館。宮崎駿の発案で, スタジオジブリ関連の展示品を多数収蔵・公開している》

- □ **GHQ** 略 連合国最高司令官総司令部（= General Headquarters）

- □ **giant** 名 ①巨人, 大男 ②巨匠 形 巨大な, 偉大な

- □ **gift** 名 ①贈り物 ②（天賦の）才能 動 授ける

- □ **gin** 名 銀

- □ **Ginza** 名 銀座《地名》

- □ **give** 動 ①与える, 贈る ②伝える, 述べる ③（～を）する **give birth to** ～を生む **give rise to** ～を引き起こす

- □ **glide** 動 ①滑る, 滑らかに動く ②静かに［こっそりと］動く

- □ **global** 形 地球（上）の, 地球規模の, 世界的な, 国際的な

- □ **globally** 副 グローバルに, 地球規模で, 世界レベルで［において］

- □ **go** 動 ①行く, 出かける ②動く ③進む, 経過する, いたる ④（ある状態に）なる **be going to** ～するつもりである **go around** 動き回る, あちらこちらに行く **go out** 外出する, 外へ出る **go out of** ～から出る［消える］ **it goes without saying** ～は言うまでもない, ～に決まっている

- □ **god** 名 神

- □ **Golden-Gai** 名（新宿）ゴールデン街《新宿区歌舞伎町にある飲食店街》

- □ **good** 形 ①よい, 上手な, 優れた, 美しい ②（数量・程度が）かなりの, 相当な **as good as** ～も同然で, ほとんど～ **be good at** ～が得意だ 副 よかった, わかった, よろしい 名 ①善, 徳, 益, 幸福 ②（-s）財産, 品, 物質

- □ **goods** 名 ①商品, 品物 ②財産, 所有物

- □ **gorgeous** 形 華麗な, 豪華な, 華やかな, すばらしい

- □ **govern** 動 治める, 管理する, 支配する

- □ **government** 名 政治, 政府, 支配

- □ **GPS** 略（= global positioning system）グローバル・ポジショニング・システム, 全地球測位システム《地球上の現在位置を測定するシステム》

- □ **grace** 動 ～を美しく飾る, 優雅にする

- □ **gradually** 副 だんだんと

□ **granny** 名〈話〉おばあちゃん, おばあさん

□ **great** 形 ①大きい, 広大な. (量や程度が)たいへんな ②偉大な, 優れた ③すばらしい, おもしろい

Great Kanto Earthquake
《the –》関東大震災《1923年9月1日午前11時58分に, 相模湾の伊豆大島を震源地として発生し, 約142,800人の死者・行方不明者を出したM7.9の大地震》

Greater Tokyo Area 《the –》大東京圏, 首都圏《東京都, 千葉県, 神奈川県, 埼玉県のほとんどを含む地域で, 2016年の統計で約3775万人が居住する世界最大の都市圏》

□ **green** 形 ①緑色の, 青々とした ②未熟な, 若い ③生き生きした 名 ①緑色 ②草地, 芝生, 野菜

□ **greet** 動 ①あいさつする ②(喜んで)迎える

□ **grew** 動 grow（成長する）の過去

□ **grief** 名 (深い)悲しみ, 悲嘆

□ **grilled** 形 グリルした, 網焼きの

□ **ground** 名 地面, 土, 土地

□ **group** 名 集団, 群 動 集まる

□ **grow to** ～するようになる

□ **grow up** 成長する

□ **grown** 動 grow（成長する）の過去分詞 形 成長した, 成人した

□ **guide** 動 (道)案内する, 導く 名 ①ガイド, 手引き, 入門書 ②案内人

H

□ **Hachi** 名 ハチ《渋谷駅まで飼い主の帰りを出迎えに行き, 飼い主の死去後も約10年にわたって待ち続けたという逸話で「忠犬」として知られる》

□ **Hachi: A Dog's Tale** 『HACHI 約束の犬』《2009年に公開されたリチャード・ギア主演のアメリカ映画》

□ **Hachiko** 名 (忠犬)ハチ公《「忠犬」として知られるハチの愛称》

□ **had** 動 have（持つ）の過去, 過去分詞 助 have の過去《過去完了の文をつくる》

□ **Hakodate** 名 函館《北海道の地名》

□ **Hakone** 名 箱根《神奈川県の地名》

□ **half** 名 半分 形 半分の, 不完全な 副 半分, なかば, 不十分に

□ **hall** 名 公会堂, ホール, 大広間, 玄関

Hama Rikyu Detached Palace 浜離宮恩賜庭園《中央区浜離宮庭園にある都立庭園》

□ **Hamamatsu-cho** 浜松町《地名》

□ **hand** 名 ①手 ②(時計の)針 ③援助の手, 助け on the other hand 一方, 他方では 動 手渡す

□ **handicraft** 名 手工芸品

□ **Haneda (Airport)** 羽田空港《大田区にある日本最大の空港の通称。正式名称は「東京国際空港」》

□ **hang** 動 〔物を～から〕つるす, 〔物を～に〕掛ける

□ **Harajuku** 名 原宿《地名》

□ **hard** 形 ①堅い ②激しい, むずかしい ③熱心な, 勤勉な ④無情な, 耐えがたい, 厳しい, きつい hard to ～し難い 副 ①一生懸命に ②激しく ③堅く

□ **hard time** つらい時期

□ **hardship** 名 ①〔欠乏によるひどい〕困難, 苦難, 困窮 ②苦難の原因, 苦労の種

□ **hardworking** 形 勤勉な, よく働く

□ **harem** 名 《イスラム教》ハーレム, 婦人部屋《転じて, 一人の男性に対して多数の女性が取り巻くような状況を指す》

□ **harvest** 名 ①収穫(物), 刈り入れ ②成果, 報い 動 収穫する

□ **has** 動 have（持つ）の3人称単数現在 助 have の3人称単数現在《現在完

了の文をつくる》

□ **have** 動①持つ, 持っている, 抱く ②(〜が)ある, いる ③食べる, 飲む ④経験する,(病気に)かかる ⑤催す, 開く ⑥(人に)〜させる **have to 〜** しなければならない 助《〈have + 過去分詞〉の形で現在完了の文をつくる》〜した, 〜したことがある, ずっと〜している

□ **he** 代 彼は[が]

□ **head** 名①頭 ②先頭 ③長, 指導者 動 向かう, 向ける **head for 〜**に向かう, 〜の方に進む

□ **headquarters** 名 本部, 司令部, 本署

□ **healthy** 形 健康な, 健全な, 健康によい

□ **hear** 動 聞く, 聞こえる

□ **heard** 動 hear (聞く) の過去, 過去分詞

□ **heart** 名①心臓, 胸 ②心, 感情, ハート ③中心, 本質

□ **held** 動 hold (つかむ) の過去, 過去分詞

□ **help** 動①助ける, 手伝う ②給仕する **help 〜 to …** 〜が…するのを助ける 名 助け, 手伝い

□ **helping** 動 help (助ける) の現在分詞 名①助力, 手助け ②(食べ物の) ひと盛り, 1杯, お代わり 形 救いの, 助けの

□ **here** 副①ここに[で] ②《-is [are] 〜》ここに〜がある ③さあ, そら 名 ここ

□ **heritage** 名 遺産, 相続財産

□ **Hibiya Line** 日比谷線《足立区の北千住駅から目黒区の中目黒駅までを結ぶ, 東京メトロが運営する路線》

□ **Higashi-ginza** 名 東銀座《中央区銀座四丁目にある, 都営地下鉄浅草線・東京メトロ日比谷線の駅名》

□ **high** 形①高い ②気高い, 高価な 副①高く ②ぜいたくに 名 高い所

□ **high-class** 形〔ホテル・レストラ

ン・店舗・品物などが〕高級な

□ **high-end** 形①〔同種類の商品の中で〕高性能の, 最高級の, ハイエンドの ②〔商品などが〕高所得者向けの, 金持ち相手の

□ **highly** 副①大いに, 非常に ②高度に, 高位に ③高く評価して, 高価で

□ **highly-trained** 形《be –》高度な訓練を受けている

□ **high-ranking** 形〔組織内の人が〕高位の, 地位の高い, 高い地位にいる

□ **high-rise** 形〔エレベーターのある〕高層[多層](ビル)の

□ **high-tech** 形①〔技術が〕ハイテクの, 先端技術の ②〔デザインが〕ハイテクの

□ **hill** 名 丘, 塚

□ **Hiroo** 名 広尾《地名》

□ **Hiroshima** 名 広島 (県・市)《地名》

□ **his** 代①彼の ②彼のもの

□ **historian** 名 歴史家, 歴史学者

□ **historic** 形 歴史上有名[重要]な, 歴史的な

□ **historical** 形 歴史の, 歴史上の, 史実に基づく

□ **historically** 副 歴史的に

□ **history** 名 歴史, 経歴

□ **hit** 動①打つ, なぐる ②ぶつける, ぶつかる ③命中する ④〔天災などが〕襲う, 打撃を与える ⑤hitの過去, 過去分詞 名①打撃 ②命中 ③大成功

□ **Hokkaido** 名 北海道

□ **hold** 動①つかむ, 持つ, 抱く ②保つ, 持ちこたえる ③収納できる, 入れることができる ④(会などを) 開く 名①つかむこと, 保有 ②支配[理解]力

□ **home** 名①家, 自国, 故郷, 家庭 ②収容所 副 家に, 自国へ **on one's way home** 帰り道で **on the way home** 帰宅途中に 形 家の, 家庭の,

地元の 動①家［本国］に帰る ②(飛行機などを)誘導する

□ **Honshu** 名 本州《島国である日本の最大の島。北海道島、四国島、九州島、付随する島とともに日本列島を構成している》

□ **horticultural** 形 園芸［植物栽培］の［に関する］

□ **hospitality** 名 歓待、温かいもてなし

□ **hot** 形①暑い、熱い ②できたての、新しい ③からい、強烈な、熱中した 副①熱く ②激しく

□ **hotel** 名 ホテル、旅館

□ **hour** 名 1時間、時間

□ **house** 名①家、家庭 ②(特定の目的のための)建物、小屋

□ **household** 名 家族、世帯 形 家族の

□ **how** 副①どうやって、どれくらい、どんなふうに ②なんて(～だろう) ③《関係副詞》～する方法

□ **however** 副 たとえ～でも 接 けれども、だが

□ **hub** 名［活動などの］中心地、拠点

□ **huge** 形 巨大な、ばく大な

□ **human** 形 人間の、人の 名 人間

□ **humidity** 名 湿度、湿気

□ **hundred** 名①100(の数字)、100人［個］ ②《-s》何百、多数 形①100の、100人［個］の ②多数の

□ **hurry** 動 急ぐ、急がせる、あわてる 名 急ぐこと、急ぐ必要

I

□ **idea** 名 考え、意見、アイデア、計画

□ **if** 接 もし～ならば、たとえ～でも、～かどうか **even if** たとえ～でも 名 疑問、条件、仮定

□ **Ikebukuro** 名 池袋《地名》

□ **illumination** 名①証明 ②《-s》イルミネーション、電飾

□ **image** 名①印象、姿 ②画像、映像 動 心に描く、想像する

□ **imagine** 動 想像する、心に思い描く

□ **imperial** 形①帝国の、皇帝の、皇后の ②荘厳なる

□ **Imperial Household Agency** 宮内庁

□ **Imperial Palace** 皇居《千代田区にある天皇の居所。江戸城跡一帯を指す》

□ **Imperial Palace East Garden** 皇居東御苑《かつての江戸城の本丸・二の丸・三の丸に位置する》

□ **important** 形 重要な、大切な、有力な

□ **Important Cultural Property** 重要文化財

□ **impressionist** 名《芸術》印象主義者

□ **impressive** 形 印象的な、深い感銘を与える

□ **in** 前①《場所・位置・所属》～(の中)に［で・の］ ②《時》～(の時)に［の・で］、～後(に)、～の間(に) ③《方法・手段》～で ④～を身につけて、～を着て ⑤～に関して、～について ⑥《状態》～の状態で **put in place** ～が導入される **step back in time** 少し前の時代に戻る 副 中へ［に］、内へ［に］

□ **incident** 名［1回だけの］出来事、［偶発的な］事件

□ **include** 動 含む、勘定に入れる

□ **including** 動 include(含む)の現在分詞 前 ～を含めて、込みで

□ **incredible** 形①信じられない、信用できない ②すばらしい、とてつもない

□ **indeed** 副①実際、本当に ②《強意》まったく 間 本当に、まさか

□ **Indian** 名①インド人 ②(アメリカ)インディアン 形①インド(人)

137

の ②(アメリカ) インディアンの

☐ **indoor** 形室内の, 屋内の

☐ **inexpensive** 形費用のかからない, 安い, あまり高価でない

☐ **influence** 名影響, 勢力 動影響をおよぼす

☐ **infrastructure** 名①〔社会の〕基盤, インフラ ②〔電気・ガス・水道・鉄道・道路などの〕生活の基礎となる設備

☐ **ingredient** 名〔特に料理の〕材料, ネタ, 原料, 含有物

☐ **inheritance** 名①相続(財産), 遺産 ②遺伝

☐ **inner** 形①内部の ②心の中の

☐ **Inner Moat** 内濠

☐ **innovation** 名①革新, 刷新 ②新しいもの, 新考案

☐ **inside** 名内部, 内側 形内部[内側]にある 副内部[内側]に 前〜の内部[内側]に

☐ **insight** 名洞察, 明察, 物事の本質を見抜くこと

☐ **inspiration** 名霊感, ひらめき, 妙案, 吸気

☐ **instance** 名①例 ②場合, 事実 **for instance** たとえば

☐ **instead** 副その代わりに **instead of** 〜の代わりに, 〜をしないで

☐ **intangible** 形①触れられない, つかみどころのない ②(財産などが)無形の

☐ **intellectual** 名知識人, 有識者, 文化人

☐ **interest** 名興味, 関心 動興味を起こさせる

☐ **interested** 動 interest (興味を起こさせる)の過去, 過去分詞 形興味を持った, 関心のある

☐ **interesting** 動 interest (興味を起こさせる)の現在分詞 形おもしろい, 興味を起こさせる

☐ **internal** 形内部の, 国内の, 本質的

な 名内部

☐ **international** 形国際(間)の

☐ **internationally** 副国際的に, 国際間で, 国際上

☐ **interrupt** 動さえぎる, 妨害する, 口をはさむ

☐ **intersection** 名交差点

☐ **into** 前①《動作・運動の方向》〜の中へ[に] ②《変化》〜に[へ]

☐ **intonation** 名イントネーション, 抑揚, 音調

☐ **involved** 動 involve (含む)の過去, 過去分詞 形①巻き込まれている, 関連する ②入り組んだ, 込み入っている

☐ **is** 動 be (〜である)の3人称単数現在

☐ **island** 名島

☐ **it** 代①それは[が], それを[に] ②《天候・日時・距離・寒暖などを示す》 **it goes without saying** 〜は言うまでもない, 〜に決まっている **It is 〜 for someone to …** (人)が…するのは〜だ

☐ **item** 名①項目, 品目 ②(新聞などの) 記事

☐ **its** 代それの, あれの

☐ **itself** 代それ自体, それ自身

☐ **izakaya** 名居酒屋

☐ **Izu Islands** 伊豆諸島《太平洋(フィリピン海)に連なる東京都の島嶼部。江戸時代, 伊豆諸島の主な有人島が, 7島であったことに由来する「伊豆七島」という呼称もある》

J

☐ **January** 名1月

☐ **Japan** 名日本《国名》

☐ **Japanese** 形日本(人・語)の 名①日本人 ②日本語

☐ **Japanese kitchen knife** 和包

138

丁

- [ ] **Japanese-style** 形 日本風の, 和式の

- [ ] **JapanTaxi** 名 ジャパンタクシー《タクシー配車用のアプリケーション》

- [ ] **Jefferson Memorial** 《the –》 ジェファーソン記念館 (Thomas Jefferson Memorial)《アメリカ合衆国の首都ワシントンD.C.にある, 第3代大統領トーマス・ジェファーソンを記念して建立された記念建造物》

- [ ] **job** 名 仕事, 職, 雇用

- [ ] **jogging** 動 jog (ジョギングする) の現在分詞 名 ジョギング

- [ ] **joren** 名 常連

- [ ] **journey** 名 ①(遠い目的地への) 旅 ②行程

- [ ] **JR (East)** JR東日本 (東日本旅客鉄道)

- [ ] **July** 名 7月

- [ ] **June** 名 6月

- [ ] **just** 形 正しい, もっともな, 当然な 副 ①まさに, ちょうど, (～した) ばかり ②ほんの, 単に, ただ～だけ ③ちょっと

- [ ] **jut** 動 突き出る

K

- [ ] **Kabuki** 名 歌舞伎

- [ ] **Kabuki-cho** 名 歌舞伎町《地名》

- [ ] **Kabuki-za** 名 歌舞伎座《中央区銀座にある歌舞伎専用の劇場》

- [ ] **Kagoshima** 名 鹿児島 (県・市)《地名》

- [ ] **Kagurazaka** 名 神楽坂《新宿区にある早稲田通りの大久保通り交差点から外堀通り交差点までの坂, および周辺の地名。江戸時代には, 外堀に設置されていた牛込門に通じる交通の要衝だった》

- [ ] **kagurazaka-dori** 名 神楽坂通り《早稲田通りのうち, 新宿区内の神楽坂下交差点～神楽坂上交差点の区間の通称》

- [ ] **kaiten-zushi** 名 回転寿司

- [ ] **kaleidoscope** 名 ①万華鏡 ②〔万華鏡のように〕千変万化するパターン [模様・場面]

- [ ] **Kamakura** 名 鎌倉《神奈川県の地名》

- [ ] **Kan'ei-ji Temple** 寛永寺《台東区上野桜木にある天台宗関東総本山の寺院。開基 (創立者) は徳川家光で, 徳川将軍家の祈祷所・菩提寺》

- [ ] **Kanagawa Prefecture** 神奈川県

- [ ] **Kanda** 名 神田《地名》

- [ ] **Kanda Myojin Shrine** 神田明神《千代田区外神田に鎮座する神社。正式名称は「神田神社」》

- [ ] **Kanda-gawa River** 神田川《東京都を流れる荒川水系の河川》

- [ ] **Kannon** 名 観音菩薩

- [ ] **Kanto Plain** 《the –》関東平野

- [ ] **Kappabashi** 名 合羽橋《台東区の浅草と上野の中間に位置する, 食器具・包材・調理器具・食品サンプル・食材・調理衣装などを一括に扱う道具専門の問屋街》

- [ ] **Keikyu Airport Line** 京急空港線《大田区の京急蒲田駅と羽田空港第1・第2ターミナル駅を結ぶ, 京浜急行電鉄 (京急) の鉄道路線》

- [ ] **Keisei Skyliner** (京成) スカイライナー《京成電鉄の京成上野駅～成田空港駅間を成田空港線 (成田スカイアクセス線) 経由で運行する特急列車の愛称》

- [ ] **kept** 動 keep (とっておく) の過去, 過去分詞

- [ ] **key** 名 ①かぎ, 手がかり ②調子 動 かぎをかける

- [ ] **kilometer** 名《長さの単位》キロメートル《略称はkm》

□ **kind** 形 親切な, 優しい 名 種類 **all kinds of** さまざまな, あらゆる種類の

□ **kishimen** 名 きしめん《幅が広く薄い日本の麺, ならびにその麺を使用した料理。一般的なうどんとは形が異なり, 平たい形状のうどんである》

□ **kit** 名 〔道具などの〕一式, 一組, セット

□ **Kitanomaru Park** 北の丸公園《千代田区の皇居に隣接する国民公園, および所在地の地名。江戸城の北の丸だった》

□ **Kiyosumi Park** 清澄庭園《江東区清澄にある都立庭園》

□ **km** 略 キロメートル《単位》

□ **knives** 名 knife（ナイフ）の複数

□ **know** 動 ①知っている, 知る, （〜が）わかる, 理解している ②知り合いである

□ **knowledge** 名 知識, 理解, 学問

□ **known** 動 know（知っている）の過去分詞 **be known as** 〜として知られている 形 知られた

□ **koban** 名 交番

□ **Kogan-ji Temple** 高岩寺《豊島区巣鴨にある曹洞宗の寺院。本尊は「とげぬき地蔵」の通称で知られる地蔵菩薩（延命地蔵）》

□ **Koganei City** 小金井市

□ **Kojimachi** 名 麹町《地名》

□ **konbini** 名 コンビニ

□ **Koraku-en Station** 後楽園駅《文京区にある東京メトロ丸ノ内線・南北線の駅》

□ **Korean** 形 韓国（人・語）の, 朝鮮（人・語）の 名 ①韓国［朝鮮］人 ②韓国［朝鮮］語

□ **Korean War** 朝鮮戦争, 韓国戦争〔韓国での呼称〕《1950–1953（休戦中）。北朝鮮（中国支援）と韓国（米主導）の戦争》

□ **Koto** 名 江東（区）《地名》

□ **Kyoto** 名 京都（府・市）《地名》

□ **Kyushu** 名 九州

L

□ **ladder** 名 はしご, はしご状のもの

□ **lake** 名 湖, 湖水, 池

□ **lamp** 名 ランプ, 灯火

□ **land** 名 ①陸地, 土地 ②国, 領域 動 上陸する, 着地する

□ **landfill** 名 埋め立て（地）, 埋め立てごみ（処理地）

□ **lantern** 名 手提げランプ, ランタン

□ **large** 形 ①大きい, 広い ②大勢の, 多量の 副 ①大きく ②自慢して

□ **large-scale** 形 大規模の

□ **largely** 副 大いに, 主として

□ **last** 《the–》最後の 副 ①最後に ②この前 名《the–》最後（のもの）, 終わり 動 続く, 持ちこたえる

□ **late** 形 ①遅い, 後期の ②最近の ③《the–》故〜 副 ①遅れて, 遅く ②最近まで, 以前

□ **later** 形 もっと遅い, もっと後の 副 で後, 後ほど

□ **latter** 形 ①後の, 末の, 後者の ②《the–》後者《代名詞的に用いる》

□ **lawn** 名 芝生

□ **layout** 名 配置, レイアウト

□ **Le Corbusier** ル・コルビュジエ《スイスで生まれ, フランスで主に活躍した建築家・画家。モダニズム建築の巨匠といわれる。1887–1965》

□ **lead** 動 ①導く, 案内する ②（生活を）送る **lead into**（ある場所）へ導く **lead to** 〜に至る, 〜に通じる, 〜を引き起こす 名 ①鉛 ②先導, 指導

□ **leader** 名 指導者, リーダー

□ **leave** 動 ①出発する, 去る ②残す, 置き忘れる ③（〜を…の）ままにしておく ④ゆだねる **leave 〜 for** …

140

…を〜のために残しておく 名①休暇 ②許可 ③別れ

- [ ] **leaves** 名 leaf（葉）の複数 動 leave（出発する）の3人称単数現在

- [ ] **led** 動 lead（導く）の過去，過去分詞

- [ ] **leg** 名①脚，すね ②支柱

- [ ] **legacy** 名〔先祖や過去からの〕伝来のもの，遺産

- [ ] **legend** 名伝説，伝説的人物，言い伝え

- [ ] **leisure** 名余暇 形余暇の

- [ ] **leisurely** 形のんびりした，くつろいだ 副のんびりと，くつろいで

- [ ] **let** 動（人に〜）させる，（〜するのを）許す，（〜をある状態に）する

- [ ] **level** 名①水平，平面 ②水準

- [ ] **life** 名①生命，生物 ②一生，生涯，人生 ③生活，暮らし，世の中

- [ ] **lifestyle** 名生活様式，ライフスタイル

- [ ] **light** 名光，明かり 形①明るい ②（色が）薄い，淡い ③軽い，容易な

- [ ] **like** 動好む，好きである 前〜に似ている，〜のような **feel like** 〜のような感じがする 形似ている，〜のような 接あたかも〜のように 名①好きなもの ②《the［one's］–》同じようなもの［人］

- [ ] **likely** 形①ありそうな，（〜）しそうな ②適当な 副たぶん，おそらく

- [ ] **line** 名①線，糸，電話線 ②（字の）行 ③列，（電車の）〜線 動①線を引く ②整列する

- [ ] **lined with** 《be –》〜が立ち並ぶ

- [ ] **link** 動①〜を結び付ける，〜をつなぐ ②〜を関連［関係］づける

- [ ] **list** 名名簿，目録，一覧表 動名簿［目録］に記入する

- [ ] **Lists of Intangible Cultural Heritage** 無形文化遺産リスト《民俗文化財，フォークロア，口承伝統などの無形文化財を保護対象とした，国際連合教育科学文化機関（ユネスコ）の事業の一つ》

- [ ] **literary** 形文学の，文芸の

- [ ] **little** 形①小さい，幼い ②少しの，短い ③ほとんど〜ない，《a –》少しはある 名少し（しか），少量 副全然〜ない，《a –》少しはある

- [ ] **livable** 形〔家・環境などが〕住みやすい，住むのに良い

- [ ] **live** 動住む，暮らす，生きている 形①生きている，生きた ②ライブの，実況の 副生で，ライブで

- [ ] **lively** 形①元気のよい，活発な ②鮮やかな，強烈な，真に迫った

- [ ] **lives** 名 life（生活）の複数

- [ ] **living** 動 live（住む）の現在分詞 名生計，生活 形①生きている，現存の ②使用されている ③そっくりの

- [ ] **local** 形①地方の，ある場所［土地］の，部分的な ②各駅停車の 名ある特定の地方のもの

- [ ] **locate** 動置く，居住する［させる］

- [ ] **location** 名位置，場所

- [ ] **locomotive** 名機関車

- [ ] **lodging** 動 lodge（泊まる）の現在分詞 名①宿泊，宿 ②《-s》下宿

- [ ] **London** 名ロンドン《英国の首都》

- [ ] **long** 形①長い，長期の ②《長さ・距離・時間などを示す語句を伴って》〜の長さ［距離・時間］ 副長い間，ずっと **long ago** ずっと前に，昔 名長い期間

- [ ] **look** 動①見る ②（〜に）見える，（〜の）顔つきをする ③注意する ④《間投詞のように》ほら，ねえ **look for** 〜を探す 名①一見，目つき ②外観，外見，様子

- [ ] **loop** 動①輪にする ②輪で囲む 名ループ，輪，輪状のもの

- [ ] **lord** 名首長，主人，領主，貴族，上院議員

- [ ] **lot** 名①くじ，運 ②地所，区画 ③たくさん，たいへん，《a – of／-s of 〜》たくさんの〜 ④やつ，連中

□ **love** 名愛, 愛情, 思いやり 動愛する, 恋する, 大好きである

□ **lover** 名 ①愛人, 恋人 ②愛好者

□ **low** 形 ①低い, 弱い ②低級の, 劣等な 副低く [点]

□ **luggage** 名旅行かばん, 手荷物

□ **lunch** 名昼食, ランチ, 軽食

□ **luxurious** 形ぜいたくな, 豪華な, 最高級の

□ **luxury** 形豪華な, 高級な, 贅沢な 名豪華さ, 贅沢(品)

M

□ **machine** 名機械, 仕掛け, 機関

□ **made** 動 make (作る) の過去, 過去分詞 **be made of** 〜でできて [作られて] いる 形作った, 作られた

□ **maglev** 略 (= magnetic levitation) 磁気浮揚, リニアモーター (カー)

□ **magnificent** 形壮大な, 壮麗な, すばらしい

□ **main** 形主な, 主要な

□ **mainly** 副主に

□ **maintain** 動 ①〔動作を〕持続 [継続] する ②〔状態を〕保つ, 保持 [維持] する ③〜を良好な状態に〕メンテナンスする, 維持する

□ **majestically** 副威厳を持って, 堂々と

□ **major** 形 ①大きいほうの, 主な, 一流の ②年長 [古参] の

□ **make** 動 ①作る, 得る ②行う, (〜に)なる ③(〜を…に)する, (〜を…)させる **make sure to** 必ず [確実に・忘れずに] 〜する

□ **making** 動 make (作る) の現在分詞 名制作, 製造

□ **male** 形男の, 雄の 名男, 雄

□ **mall** 名モール, 広場

□ **manga** 名マンガ, 日本の漫画

□ **manner** 名 ①方法, やり方 ②態度, 様子 ③《-s》行儀, 作法, 生活様式

□ **many** 形多数の, たくさんの **so many** 非常に多くの 代多数 (の人・物)

□ **map** 名地図 動 ①地図を作る ②計画を立てる

□ **March** 名3月

□ **market** 名市場, マーケット, 取引, 需要 動市場に出す

□ **marketplace** 名市場, 市がたつ広場

□ **Marunouchi** 名丸の内《地名》

□ **Marunouchi Entrance** 丸の内口《東京駅の西側にある出口。地上と地下にそれぞれ丸の内北口・丸の内中央口・丸の内南口がある》

□ **marvelous** 形驚くべき, 驚嘆すべき, すばらしい

□ **mass** 名 ①固まり, (密集した) 集まり ②多数, 多量 ③《the－es》大衆 動一団にする, 集める, 固まる

□ **mat** 名〔床に敷く〕マット

□ **match** 名試合, 勝負

□ **may** 助 ①〜かもしれない ②〜してもよい, 〜できる 名《M-》5月

□ **meal** 名 ①食事 ②ひいた粉, あらびき粉

□ **mean** 動 ①意味する ②(〜のつもりで) 言う, 意図する ③〜するつもりである

□ **meant** 動 mean (意味する) の過去, 過去分詞

□ **measure** 動 ①測る, (〜の) 寸法がある ②評価する 名 ①寸法, 測定, 計量, 単位 ②程度, 基準

□ **Mecca** 名 ①〔訪れてみたい〕憧れの地, 〔ある物事に関する〕中心的な場所, メッカ《「イスラム教の聖地」から転じて》

□ **medical** 形 ①医学の ②内科の

□ **medieval** 形中世の, 中世風の

□ **meet** 動 ①会う, 知り合いになる ②合流する, 交わる ③（条件などに）達する, 合う

□ **meeting** 動 meet（会う）の現在分詞 名 ①集まり, ミーティング, 面会 ②競技会

□ **Meguro** 名 目黒《地名》

□ **Meguro Parasitological Museum** 目黒寄生虫館《目黒区にある博物館。寄生虫に関する研究, 展示, 標本や資料の収集・鑑定, 啓蒙活動等を行う世界で唯一の寄生虫専門博物館》

□ **Meiji period** 明治時代《1868–1912》

□ **Meiji Restoration** 《the – 》明治維新

□ **Meiji-jingu Shrine** 明治神宮《渋谷区にある神社。第122代天皇の明治天皇と昭憲皇太后を御祭神とする》

□ **member** 名 一員, メンバー

□ **memorial** 名 記念物, 記録 形 記念の, 追悼の

□ **memorialize** 動 ～を記念する

□ **memory** 名 記憶（力）, 思い出

□ **men** 名 man（男性）の複数

□ **mention** 動 （～について）述べる, 言及する 名 言及, 陳述

□ **merchant** 名 商人, 貿易商

□ **meter** 名 ①メートル《長さの単位》②計量器, 計量する人

□ **metropolis** 名 首都, 大都市, メトロポリス

□ **metropolitan** 形 首都の, 大都会の 名 ①大都会の人, 都会人 ②《M-》首都大司教区の

□ **Mexican** 形 メキシコ（人）の 名 メキシコ人

□ **Michelin Guide** ミシュラン・ガイド《通例, ミシュラン社のホテル・レストラン情報誌 Red Guide を指すが, 他に旅行情報誌の Green Guide がある》

□ **mid-June** 名 6月中旬

□ **mid-November** 名 11月中旬

□ **mid-twentieth century** 20世紀半ば

□ **middle** 名 中間, 最中 in the middle of ～の真ん中［中ほど］に 形 中間の, 中央の

□ **Middle-Eastern** 形 中東の

□ **might** 助 《mayの過去》①～かもしれない ②～してもよい, ～できる 名 力, 権力

□ **mild** 形 柔和な, 温和な, 口あたりのよい, 穏やかな

□ **mile** 名 ①マイル《長さの単位。1,609m》②《-s》かなりの距離

□ **military** 形 軍隊［軍人］の, 軍事の 名 《the – 》軍, 軍部

□ **military-dominated government** 《a ～》軍部支配［主導］の政府［政権］

□ **million** 名 ①100万 ②《-s》数百万, 多数 形 ①100万の ②多数の

□ **mind** 名 ①心, 精神, 考え ②知性

□ **minister** 名 ①大臣, 閣僚, 公使 ②聖職者

□ **Ministry of Defence** 防衛省《当時は「防衛庁」》

□ **minor** 形 ①少数の, 小さい［少ない］方の ②重要でない

□ **mint** 動 《貨幣を》鋳造する

□ **minute** 名 ①（時間の）分 ②ちょっとの間 形 ごく小さい, 細心の

□ **miraculously** 副 驚異的に, 奇跡的に

□ **miso** 名 味噌

□ **miss** 動 ①失敗する, 免れる, ～を見逃す, （目標を）はずす ②（～が）ないのに気づく, （人が）いなくてさびしく思う

□ **mistake** 名 誤り, 誤解, 間違い 動 間違える, 誤解する

□ **Mitaka City** 三鷹市

□ **mix** 動①混ざる, 混ぜる ②(～を) 一緒にする 名混合(物)

□ **Miyazaki Hayao** 宮崎駿《日本の映画監督, アニメーター, 漫画家で,「三鷹の森ジブリ美術館」館主。1941–》

□ **moat** 名堀

□ **model** 名①模型, 設計図 ②模範 形模範の, 典型的な 動(～をもとにして)作る, 模型を作る

□ **modern** 形現代[近代]の, 現代的な, 最近の 名現代[近代]人

□ **modern-day** 形現代の, 今日の

□ **modernization** 名近代[現代]化

□ **money** 名金, 通貨 save money コストを削減する, 貯金する

□ **monster** 名怪物

□ **month** 名月, 1ヵ月

□ **Monzen-machi** 名門前町《有力な寺院・神社の門前に形成された商工業町のこと》

□ **more** 形①もっと多くの ②それ以上の, 余分の 副もっと, さらに多く, いっそう more of ～よりもっと more than ～以上 名もっと多くの物[人]

□ **moreover** 副その上, さらに

□ **mori-soba** 名盛りそば《そばの食べ方の一つ。ゆでて水にさらして締め, せいろなどに盛りつけたそばを, そばつゆにつけながら食べる》

□ **morning** 名朝, 午前

□ **most** 形①最も多い ②たいていの, 大部分の 代①大部分, ほとんど ②最多数, 最大限 副最も(多く)

□ **mountain** 名①山 ②《the ～ M-s》～山脈 ③山のようなもの, 多量

□ **mountainous** 形①山の多い, 山地の ②〔山のように〕巨大な

□ **move** 動①動く, 動かす ②感動させる ③引っ越す, 移動する move

around あちこち移動する move to ～に引っ越す 名①動き, 運動 ②転居, 移動

□ **moving** 動move（動く）の現在分詞 形①動いている ②感動させる

□ **Mt. Fuji** 富士山

□ **much** 形(量・程度が)多くの, 多量の 副①とても, たいへん ②《比較級・最上級を修飾して》ずっと, はるかに 名多量, たくさん, 重要なもの

□ **museum** 名博物館, 美術館

□ **Museum of Yebisu Beer** エビスビール記念館《渋谷区恵比寿にある, エビスビール(サッポロビールが製造・販売する麦芽100%ビールの商標)のギャラリー。会社の歴史を紹介する展示やツアー, ビールの試飲がある》

□ **must-see** 名〈話〉必見のもの

N

□ **Naito-Shinjuku** 名内藤新宿《江戸時代に設けられた宿場の一つ。甲州街道の宿場のうち, 江戸日本橋から数えて最初の宿場。現在の新宿区新宿一丁目から二丁目・三丁目の一帯にあたる》

□ **name** 名①名前 ②名声 動①名前をつける ②名指しする

□ **Nara** 名奈良(県・市)《地名》

□ **Narita (International Airport)** 成田国際空港《千葉県成田市にある日本最大の国際拠点空港》

□ **Narita Express** 成田エクスプレス《JR東日本が, 大船駅・横浜駅・高尾駅・大宮駅・池袋駅・新宿駅・品川駅～成田空港駅間で運行する特別急行列車》

□ **narrow** 形①狭い ②限られた 動狭くなる[する]

□ **nation** 名国, 国家, 《the – 》国民

□ **national** 形国家[国民]の, 全国の

□ **National Museum** 国立博物館
《独立行政法人・国立文化財機構が運
営する博物館。東京（台東区上野）・京
都（京都市）・奈良（奈良市）・九州（太
宰府市）にある》

□ **National Museum of
Emerging Science and
Innovation Miraikan** 日本科
学未来館《江東区青海の国際研究交流
大学村内にある科学館。最新テクノロ
ジーや地球環境, 宇宙, 生命の不思議
についての展示・体験がある》

□ **National Museum of
Western Art** 国立西洋美術館《台
東区の上野公園内にある, 西洋の美術
作品を専門とする美術館。「ル・コルビ
ュジエの建築作品-近代建築運動への
顕著な貢献-」の構成資産として, 世界
文化遺産に登録されている》

□ **National Theater** 国立劇場《千
代田区にある劇場で, 日本の伝統芸能
を上演するほか, 伝承者の養成や調査
研究も行っている》

□ **National Treasure** 国宝《文化
財保護法によって国が指定した有形
文化財（重要文化財）のうち, 世界文
化の見地から価値が高く, 類いない国
民の宝たるものとして国（文部科学大
臣）が指定したもの》

□ **natural** 形①自然の, 天然の ②生
まれつきの, 天性の ③当然な

□ **navigate** 動航行する, 飛行する

□ **near** 前～の近くに, ～のそばに 形
近い, 親しい 副近くに, 親密で

□ **nearby** 形近くの, 間近の 副近く
で, 間近で

□ **nearly** 副①近くに, 親しく ②ほと
んど, あやうく

□ **need** 動（～を）必要とする, 必要で
ある **need to do** ～する必要がある
助～する必要がある 名①必要（性），
《-s》必要なもの ②まさかの時

□ **neighborhood** 名近所（の人々），
付近

□ **neon** 名ネオン

□ **nestle** 動〔家などが～に囲まれた〕
快適な場所にいる

□ **network** 名回路, 網状組織, ネッ
トワーク

□ **new** 形①新しい, 新規の ②新鮮な,
できたての

□ **New York (City)** 《米》ニューヨ
ーク市

□ **next** 形①次の, 翌～ ②隣の 副①
次に ②隣に **next to** ～のとなりに,
～の次に 代次の人［もの］

□ **Nezu** 名根津《地名》

□ **Nezu Museum** 根津美術館《港
区南青山にある私立美術館。実業家の
初代根津嘉一郎が所蔵した日本・東洋
の古美術品コレクションを保存・展
示している》

□ **nice** 形すてきな, よい, きれいな,
親切な

□ **nicely** 副①うまく, よく ②上手に,
親切に, 几帳面に

□ **night** 名夜, 晩

□ **nightclub** 名ナイトクラブ

□ **nightlife** 名夜の娯楽, 夜遊び

□ **nigiri-zushi** 名握り寿司

□ **Nihonbashi** 名日本橋《地名》

□ **Nihonbashi Bridge** 日本橋《中
央区の日本橋川に架かる国道の橋で,
国の重要文化財。日本の道路元標があ
り, 日本の道路網の始点となってい
る》

□ **Nijubashi (Bridge)** 二重橋《皇
居内にある橋の通称で, 皇居正門から
長和殿へ向かう途上, 二重橋濠に架か
る鉄橋のこと。本来の名称は「正門鉄
橋（せいもんてつばし）」》

□ **Nikko** 名日光《栃木県の地名》

□ **Nikko Toshogu** 日光東照宮《栃
木県日光市に所在する神社で, 江戸幕
府初代将軍・徳川家康を神格化した東
照大権現（とうしょうだいごんげん）
を主祭神として祀る》

□ **nine** 名9（の数字）, 9人［個］ 形9の,

9人［個］の

- □ **Ninomaru Teien** 二の丸庭園《皇居東御苑に位置する庭園。江戸城の二の丸がある之》

- □ **Nippori Station** 日暮里駅《荒川区西日暮里にある。JR東日本・京成電鉄・東京都交通局の駅》

- □ **no** 副 ①いいえ，いや ②少しも〜ない 形〜がない，少しも〜ない，〜どころでない，〜禁止 名 否定，拒否

- □ **noodle** 名 麺類，ヌードル

- □ **normally** 副 普通は，通常は

- □ **north** 名《the – 》北，北部 形 北の，北からの 副 北へ［に］，北から

- □ **northern** 形 北の，北向きの，北からの

- □ **northwest** 名 北西（部）形 北西の，北西向きの 副 北西へ，北西から

- □ **northwestern** 形 北西の，北西からの

- □ **not** 副 〜でない，〜しない not only 〜 but（also）… 〜だけでなく…もまた

- □ **nothing** 代 何も〜ない［しない］

- □ **notice** 名 ①注意 ②通知 ③公告 動 ①気づく，認める ②通告する

- □ **November** 名 11月

- □ **now** 副 ①今（では），現在 ②今すぐに ③では，さて 名 今，現在 形 今の，現在の

- □ **nowadays** 副 このごろは，現在では

- □ **number** 名 ①数，数字，番号 ②〜号，〜番 ③《-s》多数 a number of いくつかの〜，多くの〜 動 番号をつける，数える

- □ **numerous** 形 多数の

- □ **NY** 略《米》ニューヨーク

O

- □ **oasis** 名 オアシス，憩いの場

- □ **observation** 名 観察（力），注目

- □ **observe** 動 ①観察［観測］する，監視［注視］する ②気づく ③守る，遵守する

- □ **occasion** 名 ①場合，（特定の）時 ②機会，好機 ③理由，根拠

- □ **occupy** 動 ①占領する，保有する ②居住する ③占める ④（職に）つく，従事する

- □ **Oda Nobunaga** 織田信長《豊臣秀吉・徳川家康とともに「三英傑」の一人として知られる戦国大名。1534–1582》

- □ **Odaiba** 名 お台場《地名》

- □ **Oedo Line** 大江戸線《東京都交通局が運営する鉄道路線（都営地下鉄）。練馬区の光が丘駅と新宿区の都庁前駅を結ぶ放射部と，都庁前駅から各地を経由して同駅に至る環状部から構成される》

- □ **of** 前 ①《所有・所属・部分》〜の，〜に属する ②《性質・特徴・材料》〜の，〜製の ③《部分》〜のうち ④《分離・除去》〜から of which 〜の中で

- □ **off** 副 ①離れて ②はずれて ③止まって ④休んで get off（〜から）降りる 形 ①離れて ②季節はずれの ③休みの 前 〜を離れて，〜をはずれて，（値段が）〜引きの

- □ **offer** 動 申し出る，申し込む，提供する 名 提案，提供

- □ **office** 名 ①会社，事務所，職場，役所，局 ②官職，地位，役

- □ **official** 形 ①公式の，正式の ②職務上の，公の 名 公務員，役人，職員

- □ **officially** 副 公式に，職務上，正式に

- □ **often** 副 しばしば，たびたび

- □ **Ogasawara Islands** 小笠原諸島《東京都小笠原村の行政区域。東京都特別区の南南東約1,000kmの太平洋上にある30余りの島々からなる。別名「ボニン諸島」》

- □ **Oku** 奥《武家の邸宅における日

常生活の場。対義語は, 儀礼や政治の
場である「表」》

- **old** 形①年取った, 老いた ②〜歳
の ③古い, 昔の 名昔, 老人

- **old-fashioned** 形時代遅れの, 旧
式な

- **olden** 形〈文〉昔の

- **Omiya** 名大宮《埼玉県の地名》

- **Omoide-yokocho** 名思い出横
丁《新宿区にある「新宿西口商店街」
の別名》

- **Omote** 名表《武家の邸宅における
儀礼や政治の場。対義語は, 日常生活
の場である「奥」》

- **Omote-sando** 名表参道《明治神
宮の参道の一つで, 現在の都道413号
線のうち, 青山通り〜神宮橋交差点ま
での区間。また, その周囲から地下鉄・
表参道駅周辺までを含む一帯の総称》

- **on** 前①《場所・接触》〜（の上）に
②《日・時》〜に, 〜と同時に, 〜のす
ぐ後で ③《関係・従事》〜に関して,
〜について, 〜して **on one's way
home** 帰り道で **on one's way to 〜**
に行く途中で **on the other hand** 一
方, 他方では **on the way home** 帰
宅途中に 副①身につけて, 上に ②
前へ, 続けて **get on**（電車などに）乗
る

- **once** 副①一度, 1回 ②かつて 名
一度, 1回 接いったん〜すると

- **one** 名1《人[個]》one ②《個》one of
〜の1つ[人] 形①1《人[個]》の
②ある〜 ③《the −》唯一の **from
one side to the other** 一方の側から
他の側へ 代①（一般の）人, ある物
②一方, 片方 ③〜なもの **on one's
way home** 帰り道で **on one's way
to 〜**に行く途中で

- **only** 形唯一の 副①単に, 〜にす
ぎない, ただ〜だけ ②やっと **not
only 〜 but（also）**… 〜だけでなく
…もまた 接ただし, だがしかし

- **O-oku** 名大奥《江戸時代に存在した
将軍家の子女や正室, 奥女中（御殿女
中）たちの居所》

- **open** 形①開いた, 広々とした ②
公開された 動①開く, 始まる ②広
がる, 広げる ③打ち明ける **open up
to the world** 世界に門戸を開く, 対
外開放する

- **open air** 戸外, 野外

- **opera** 名歌劇, オペラ

- **operate** 動①（機械などが）動く,
運転する, 管理する, 操業する ②作
用する ③手術する

- **opposite** 形反対の, 向こう側の
前〜の向こう側に 名反対の人[物]

- **option** 名①選ぶこと, 選択（する
こと）②選択の自由[権利] ③選択肢,
選択した[できる]もの

- **or** 接①〜か…, または ②さもない
と ③すなわち, 言い換えると **or so**
〜かそこらで

- **order** 名①順序 ②整理, 整頓 ③
命令, 注文（品）**in order to 〜**する
ために, 〜しようと 動①注文する ②整頓する, 整
理する

- **ordinary** 形①普通の, 通常の ②
並の, 平凡な

- **organization** 名組織（化）, 編成,
団体, 機関

- **origin** 名起源, 出自

- **original** 形①始めの, 元の, 本来の
②独創的な 名原型, 原文

- **originally** 副①元は, 元来 ②独創
的に

- **originate** 動始まる, 始める, 起こ
す, 生じる

- **Osaka** 名大阪（府・市）,（江戸時代
までの）大坂《地名》

- **Oshiage** 名押上《地名》

- **oshiya** 名押し屋《鉄道の朝夕のラ
ッシュ時に, 列車の扉に挟まりかかっ
た乗客や荷物を車内に押し込む人》

- **Ota Dokan** 太田道灌《室町時代後
期の武将。江戸城を築城したことで有
名。1432–1486》

147

- **Ota Memorial Museum of Art** 太田記念美術館《渋谷区にある浮世絵専門の私設美術館》
- **otaku** 图オタク
- **Otemachi** 图大手町《地名》
- **Otemon Gate** 大手門《江戸城の三ノ丸大手門および西ノ丸大手門》
- **other** 形①ほかの, 異なった ②(2つのうち) もう一方の, (3つ以上のうち) 残りの **on the other hand** 一方, 他方では 代①ほかの人 [物] ②《the -》残りの1つ **each other** お互いに **from one side to the other** 一方の側から他の側へ **than any other** ほかのどの~よりも 副そうでなく, 別に
- **out** 副①外へ [に], 不在で, 離れて ②世に出て ③消えて ④すっかり **go out** 外出する, 外へ出る **go out of** ~から出る [消える] **out of** ~から作り出して, ~を材料として **spread out** 広げる, 展開する **stretch out** 手足を伸ばす, 背伸びする **turn out** (結局~に) なる 形①外の, 遠く離れた ②公表された 前~から外へ [に] 動①追い出す ②露見する ③ (スポーツで) アウトにする
- **outer** 形外の, 外側の
- **Outer Moat** 外濠
- **outside** 图外部, 外側 形外部の, 外側の 副外へ, 外側に 前~の外に [で・の・へ], ~の範囲を越えて
- **outskirt** 图はずれ, 郊外《都市または町の中で中心から遠く離れた所》
- **over** 前①~の上の [に], ~を一面に覆って ②~を越えて, ~以上に, ~よりまさって ③~の向こう側の [に] ④~の間 **all over** ~中で, 全体に亘って, ~の至る所で, 全て終わって, もうだめで **all over the world** 世界中に 副上に, 一面に, ずっと **rule over** 治める, 統御する **take over** 引き継ぐ, 支配する, 乗っ取る 形①上部の, 上位の, 過多の ②終わって, すんで
- **overcome** 動勝つ, 打ち勝つ, 克

服する **be overcome with** ~に圧倒される, ~にやられる
- **overnight** 副一晩中, 夜通し 图一泊旅行 形①夜通しの ②一泊の
- **overseas** 形海外の, 外国の 副海外へ 图国外
- **overthrown** 動 overthrow (ひっくり返す) の過去分詞
- **overview** 图概観, 大要, あらまし
- **overwhelm** 動 [精神的・感情的に人を] 圧倒する, 打ちのめす
- **own** 形自身の 動持っている, 所有する
- **owner** 图持ち主, オーナー
- **ownership** 图所有者, 所有権

P

- **pack** 動①[人が場所に] 群がる, 満員になる ②[物が集まって] かたまる
- **paid** 動 pay (払う) の過去, 過去分詞 形有給の, 支払い済みのの
- **pair** 图 (2つから成る) 一対, 一組, ペア 動対になる [する]
- **palace** 图宮殿, 大邸宅
- **paradise** 图①天国 ②地上の楽園
- **parasitological** 形寄生虫学の
- **Paris** 图パリ《フランスの首都》
- **park** 图①公園, 広場 ②駐車場 動駐車する
- **part** 图①部分, 割合 ②役目 動分ける, 分かれる, 別れる
- **particular** 形①特別の ②詳細な 图事項, 細部, 《-s》詳細 **in particular** 特に, とりわけ
- **particularly** 副特に, とりわけ
- **partly** 副一部分は, ある程度は
- **party** 图①パーティー, 会, 集まり ②派, 一行, 隊, 一味
- **PASMO** 图パスモ《株式会社パス

モが発行し, 関東地方・山梨県・静岡県の鉄道事業者・バス事業者が発売する, 電子マネー機能を備えたICカード乗車券》

□ **pass** 動①過ぎる, 通る ②(年月が)たつ ③(試験に)合格する ④手渡す **pass away** 過ぎ去る, 終わる, 死ぬ **pass through** 〜を通る, 通行する 名①通過 ②入場券, 通行許可 ③合格, パス

□ **passenger** 名乗客, 旅客

□ **passersby** 名通行人, 通り掛かり[すがり]の人《passerbyの複数形》

□ **past** 形過去の, この前の 名過去(の出来事) 前《時間・場所》〜を過ぎて, 〜を越して 副通り越して, 過ぎて

□ **path** 名①(踏まれてできた)小道, 歩道 ②進路, 通路

□ **patiently** 副我慢強く, 根気よく

□ **pay** 動①支払う, 払う, 報いる, 償う ②割に合う, ペイする 名給料, 報い

□ **peace** 名①平和, 和解,《the – 》治安 ②平穏, 静けさ

□ **peak** 名頂点, 最高点 動最高になる, ピークに達する

□ **people** 名①(一般に)人々 ②民衆, 世界の人々, 国民, 民族 ③人間

□ **per** 前〜につき, 〜ごとに

□ **percent** 名パーセント, 百分率

□ **performance** 名①実行, 行為 ②成績, できばえ, 業績 ③演劇, 演奏, 見世物

□ **perhaps** 副たぶん, ことによると

□ **period** 名①期, 期間, 時代 ②ピリオド, 終わり

□ **Perry** 名《Commodore – 》ペリー提督《マシュー・カルブレイス・ペリー(Matthew Calbraith Perry)アメリカ海軍の軍人, 1794–1858》

□ **photocopy** 名写真複写, コピー, コピー印刷 動〜を複写する, コピーする

□ **picnic** 名ピクニック 動ピクニックに行く

□ **picturesque** 形絵のような

□ **piece** 名①一片, 部分 ②1個, 1本 ③作品 **piece by piece** 一つ一つ

□ **pine** 名マツ(松), マツ材

□ **place** 名①場所, 建物 ②余地, 空間 ③《one's – 》家, 部屋 **put in place** 〜が導入される **take place** 行われる, 起こる 動①置く, 配置する ②任命する, 任じる

□ **plan** 名計画, 設計(図), 案 動計画する

□ **planet** 名惑星, 遊星

□ **plastic** 形①プラスチック(製)の ②造形の, 塑像の 名プラスチック, ビニール,《-s》プラスチック製品

□ **plate** 名①(浅い)皿, 1皿の料理 ②金属板, 標札, プレート 動めっきする, 板金をする

□ **play** 動①遊ぶ, 競技する ②(楽器を)演奏する, (役を)演じる 名遊び, 競技, 劇

□ **playhouse** 名①劇場 ②《遊具》子どもの家

□ **pleasant** 形①(物事が)楽しい, 心地よい ②快活な, 愛想のよい

□ **pleasantly** 副楽しく, 心地よく

□ **pleasure** 名喜び, 楽しみ, 満足, 娯楽

□ **point** 名①先, 先端 ②点 ③地点, 時点, 箇所 ④《the – 》要点, 核心 動①(〜を)指す, 向ける ②とがらせる

□ **police** 名①《the – 》警察, 警官 ②公安, 治安 動警備する, 治安を維持する

□ **policy** 名政策, 方針, 手段

□ **political** 形①政治の, 政党の ②策略的な

□ **politically** 副政治上, 政治的に

□ **pond** 名池

□ **popular** 形①人気のある, 流行の ②一般的な, 一般向きの **be popular**

with ～に人気がある

□ **popular culture** 大衆文化［ポップカルチャー］

□ **populated** 形住民のいる，人口の多い

□ **population** 名人口，住民（数）

□ **pork** 名豚肉

□ **port** 名①港，港町，空港 ②ポートワイン

□ **portable** 形持ち運びのできる，ポータブルな

□ **possible** 形①可能な ②ありうる，起こりうる

□ **post-war** 形戦後の，戦争後の

□ **post-work** 形仕事後の

□ **posture** 名〔立っているときの人の〕身のこなし，立ち振る舞い

□ **potato** 名ジャガイモ

□ **power** 名力，能力，才能，勢力，権力

□ **powerful** 形力強い，実力のある，影響力のある

□ **practical** 形①実際的な，実用的な，役に立つ ②経験を積んだ

□ **practically** 副①事実上，実質的に ②ほとんど

□ **preceding** 動precede（先行する）の現在分詞 形先行する，先立つ，前の

□ **prefecture** 名県，府

□ **prefer** 動（～のほうを）好む，（～のほうが）よいと思う

□ **premier** 名首相，総理大臣

□ **prepaid** 形プリペイドの，前払いの

□ **prepare** 動①準備［用意］をする ②覚悟する［させる］

□ **prepared** 形準備［用意］のできた

□ **present** 形現在の 名《the－》現在

□ **present-day** 形今日の，現代の，

この頃の

□ **preserve** 動保存［保護］する，保つ

□ **preview** 名下見

□ **price** 名①値段，代価 ②《-s》物価，相場 動値段をつける，値段を聞く

□ **priced** 形価格［定価］の付けられた

□ **priceless** 形とても高価な，金では買えない

□ **printing** 動print（印刷する）の現在分詞 名印刷，焼き付け

□ **privacy** 名（干渉されない）自由な生活，プライバシー

□ **private** 形①私的な，個人の ②民間の，私立の ③内密の，人里離れた

□ **privately** 副内密に，非公式に，個人的に

□ **problem** 名問題，難問

□ **proceed** 動①〔行為を〕始める，開始する ②〔ある方向へ〕進む，前進する

□ **proclaim** 動〔正式に〕～を公表［宣言・宣告］する

□ **produce** 動①生産する，製造する ②生じる，引き起こす 名①生産額［物］②結果

□ **product** 名①製品，産物 ②成果，結果

□ **professional** 形専門の，プロの，職業的な 名専門家，プロ

□ **professor** 名教授，師匠

□ **progress** 名①進歩，前進 ②成り行き，経過 動前進する，上達する

□ **prohibit** 動①〔法令などで人が～するのを〕禁止する，差し止める ②〔人が～するのを〕妨げる，邪魔をする

□ **project** 名計画，プロジェクト

□ **property** 名①財産，所有物［地］②性質，属性

□ **prosper** 動①〔事業などが〕成功する ②繁栄する，力強く成長する

□ **protect** 動保護する，防ぐ

□ **protection** 图保護, 保護するもの〔人〕

□ **provide** 動①供給する, 用意する, (～に)備える ②規定する

□ **proximity** 图〔時間・空間・関係の〕近いこと, 近接

□ **pub** 图酒場, パブ

□ **public** 图一般の人々, 大衆 形公の, 公開の

□ **public viewing** パブリックビューイング, 一般公開

□ **puppet** 图操り人形, 指人形, 手先

□ **purchase** 動購入する, 獲得する 图購入(物), 仕入れ, 獲得

□ **pure** 形①純粋な, 混じりけのない ②罪のない, 清い

□ **push** 動①押す, 押し進む, 押し進める ②進む, 突き出る 图押し, 突進, 後援

□ **pusher** 图押す人〔物・道具〕

□ **put** 動①置く, のせる ②入れる, つける ③(ある状態に)する ④putの過去, 過去分詞 **put in place** ～が導入される

Q

□ **quaint** 形風変わりな, 珍しい

□ **quarter** 图①4分の1, 25セント, 15分, 3カ月 ②方面, 地域 ③部署 動4等分する

□ **question** 图質問, 疑問, 問題 動①質問する ②調査する ③疑う

□ **quick** 形(動作が)速い, すばやい 副速く, 急いで, すぐに

□ **quickly** 副敏速に, 急いで

□ **quiet** 形①静かな, 穏やかな, じっとした ②おとなしい, 無口な, 目立たない 图静寂, 平穏 動静まる, 静める

□ **quietly** 副①静かに ②平穏に, 控えめに

R

□ **radio** 图①ラジオ ②無線電話[電報] 動放送する

□ **rail** 图①横木, 手すり ②レール, 鉄道

□ **railway** 图鉄道

□ **Rainbow Bridge** レインボーブリッジ《港区芝浦地区と台場地区(港区台場および江東区有明)を結ぶ吊り橋の愛称。正式名称は「東京港連絡橋」》

□ **rainy** 形雨降りの, 雨の多い

□ **ramen** 图ラーメン

□ **ramen-ya** 图ラーメン屋

□ **range** 图列, 連なり, 範囲 動①並ぶ, 並べる ②およぶ

□ **rank** 图①列 ②階級, 位 動①並ぶ, 並べる ②分類する

□ **rapidly** 副速く, 急速, すばやく, 迅速に

□ **rare** 形①まれな, 珍しい, 逸品の ②希薄な

□ **raw** 形①生の, 未加工の ②未熟な 图生もの

□ **reach** 動①着く, 到着する, 届く ②手を伸ばして取る 图手を伸ばすこと, (手の)届く範囲

□ **ready-to-eat** 形インスタントの, 〔料理などが〕食べられる状態になっている

□ **real** 形実際の, 実在する, 本物の 副本当に

□ **real-life** 形①現実の[に起きている], 実際の ②〔人物などが〕実在の

□ **really** 副本当に, 実際に, 確かに

□ **reason** 图①理由 ②理性, 道理 動①推論する ②説き伏せる

□ **reasonable** 形筋の通った, 分別のある

□ **reasonably** 副分別よく, 賢明に, 適当に

□ **rebuilt** 動rebuild(再建する)の過

去, 過去分詞

- **receive** 動 ①〔与えられた物を〕受け取る, 受理する ②〔知らせや情報を〕聞く, 知る ③〔手紙や電話を〕もらう, 受ける ④〔称号などを〕受ける, 授与される
- **recent** 形 近ごろの, 近代の
- **recently** 副 近ごろ, 最近
- **rechargeable** 形 再充電〔補充〕可能な
- **reclaim** 動 ①〜を再要求する, 取り戻す ②〜を埋め立てる, 開墾する ③〜を再生する, 再利用する
- **recognition** 名 承認, 表彰, お礼
- **recognize** 動 認める, 認識〔承認〕する
- **recommendation** 名 ①推薦(状) ②勧告
- **reconstruction** 名 再建, 復興, 復元
- **recover** 動 正常な状態に戻す, 〔失ったもの・損失を〕取り戻す, 回復する
- **red** 形 赤い 名 赤, 赤色
- **red-brick** 形 赤れんが(造り)の
- **refer** 動 ①〔〜を…に〕差し向ける, 持ち込む ②〔〜を…に〕参照させる ③〔問題の解決などを…に〕委託する ④〔〜を…に〕属するものとする ⑤〔〜の原因を…に〕帰する, 〔〜を…の〕せいにする
- **refined** 動 refine（純化する）の過去, 過去分詞 形 精製された, 上品な, 洗練された
- **reflect** 動 ①〜を反射する, 反響する ②〜を映す, 示す, 反映する
- **regarding** 動 regard（見なす）の現在分詞 前 〜に関しては, 〜について
- **region** 名 ①地方, 地域 ②範囲
- **regular** 形 ①規則的な, 秩序のある ②定期的な, 一定の, 習慣的な
- **regularly** 副 整然と, 規則的に

- **relatively** 副 比較的, 相対的に
- **remain** 動 ①残っている, 残る ②（〜の）ままである〔いる〕 名《-s》①残り(もの) ②遺跡
- **remaining** 動 remain（残っている）の現在分詞 形 残った, 残りの
- **remarkable** 形 ①異常な, 例外的な ②注目に値する, すばらしい
- **rename** 動《rename A B》Aの名前をBに変える〔付け替える〕, AをBに改名〔改称〕する
- **replacement** 名 取り替え, 交換, 置換
- **representative** 名 ①代表(者), 代理人 ②代議士 ③典型, 見本 形 ①代表の, 代理の ②典型的な
- **reproduction** 名 複製〔復元・再現〕すること
- **reputation** 名 評判, 名声, 世評
- **require** 動 ①必要とする, 要する ②命じる, 請求する
- **reserve** 動 〜を用意しておく, 予約する, 取っておく, 予定しておく
- **reside** 動 〔場所に〕住む, 居住する, 駐在する
- **residence** 名 住宅, 居住
- **resident** 名〔特定の場所に長期間住む〕居住者
- **resort** 名 行楽地, リゾート
- **respectively** 副 それぞれに, めいめい
- **rest** 名 ①休息 ②安静 ③休止, 停止 ④《the −》残り
- **restaurant** 名 レストラン, 料理店, 食堂
- **restoration** 名 ①回復, 復活, 修復 ②《the R-》王政復古
- **result** 名 結果, 成り行き, 成績 動 （結果として）起こる, 生じる, 結局〜になる
- **retail** 形 小売りの 名 小売り(店)
- **retain** 動 ①〜を持ち続ける, 〜を

保っている ②～を覚えている，～を
心に留める ③〔ある場所に-・を〕と
どめて［ためて］おく

□ **retainer** 名①リテーナ，固定器具
②〔長期の〕雇用者〔雇われる人〕，従
業員 ③〔騎士や貴族などに使えた〕
家臣，家来，郎党

□ **retro-type** 形古風な，レトロな

□ **return** 動帰る，戻る，返す

□ **reunify** 動〔分割されたもの・国な
どを〕再結合［再統一］する

□ **revel** 動大いに楽しむ，非常に喜ぶ，
享楽する

□ **revolving** 動 revolve（回転する）
の現在分詞 形回転する，回転式の
名回転

□ **rhythm** 名リズム，調子，(韻)律

□ **rice** 名米，飯

□ **rich** 形①富んだ，金持ちの ②豊か
な，濃い，深い 名裕福な人

□ **Richard Gere** リチャード・ギア
《アメリカ合衆国の俳優。1949–》

□ **ride** 動乗る，乗って行く，馬に乗る
名乗ること

□ **right** 形①正しい ②適切な ③健全
な ④右(側)の 副①まっすぐに，す
ぐに ②右(側)に ③ちょうど，正確
に

□ **rigid** 形①硬い，固定した ②融通の
きかない

□ **Rikugi-en** 名六義園《文京区にあ
る都立庭園。徳川5代将軍・綱吉の側
用人であった柳沢吉保が，自らの下屋
敷として造営した大名庭園》

□ **rise** 動①昇る，上がる ②生じる
名①上昇，上がること ②発生 **give
rise to** ～を引き起こす

□ **river** 名①川 ②(溶岩などの)大量
流出

□ **road** 名①道路，道，通り ②手段，
方法

□ **robe** 名〔家庭用の〕(バス)ローブ，
ドレッシング・ガウン

□ **role** 〔劇や映画などの〕役，役柄

□ **romantic** 形ロマンチックな，空
想的な 名ロマンチックな人

□ **Rome** 名①ローマ《イタリアの首
都》②古代ローマ(帝国)

□ **room** 名①部屋 ②空間，余地

□ **root** 名①根，根元 ②根源，原因 ③
《-s》先祖，ルーツ 動根づかせる，根
づく

□ **Roppongi** 名六本木《地名》

□ **Roppongi Crossing** 六本木交
差点

□ **Roppongi Hills** 六本木ヒルズ

□ **Roppongi Station** 六本木駅
《港区にある東京メトロ日比谷線・都
営地下鉄大江戸線の駅》

□ **rose** 名①バラ(の花) ②バラ色
形バラ色の 動 rise（昇る）の過去

□ **route** 名道，道筋，進路，回路

□ **rubber-wheeled** 名ラバー砥石
の

□ **rule over** 治める，統御する

□ **ruled** 名①規則，ルール ②支配
動支配する

□ **ruling** 動 rule（支配する）の現在
分詞 形支配的な，優勢な 名①裁定，
決定 ②支配

□ **run** 動①走る ②運行する ③(川が)
流れる ④経営する

□ **rush** 動突進する，せき立てる 名突
進，突撃，殺到

□ **Russia** 名ロシア《国名》

□ **rye** 名ライ麦

□ **Ryogoku** 名両国《地名》

□ **Ryogoku Kokugikan** 両国国
技館《墨田区横網一丁目にある大相撲
の興行のための施設》

□ **Ryogoku Station** 両国駅《墨田
区横網一丁目にある，JR東日本中央・
総武線・都営地下鉄大江戸線の駅》

S

- [ ] **safe** 形 ①安全な, 危険のない ②用心深い, 慎重な 名 金庫

- [ ] **safety** 名 安全, 無事, 確実

- [ ] **Saitama Prefecture** 埼玉県

- [ ] **sake** 名 日本酒

- [ ] **Sakuradamon Gate** 桜田門 《江戸城の内濠に造られた門の一つ》

- [ ] **salaried** 形 ①〔人が〕月給取りの, サラリーマンの ②〔地位や時間が〕有給の

- [ ] **salary** 名 給料

- [ ] **same** 形 ①同じ, 同様の ②前述の 代 《the –》同一の人[物] 副 《the –》同様に

- [ ] **samurai** 名 侍

- [ ] **Samurai Museum** サムライミュージアム《新宿区歌舞伎町にある体験型ミュージアム。鎧兜を身に着けたり殺陣ショーにも参加できる》

- [ ] **sandwich** 名 サンドイッチ 動 間にはさむ, 挿入する

- [ ] **save** 動 ①救う, 守る ②とっておく, 節約する **save money** コストを削減する, 貯金する

- [ ] **say** 動 言う, 口に出す **it goes without saying** ~は言うまでもない, ~に決まっている 名 言うこと, 言い分

- [ ] **scandalous** 形 あきれるような, みっともない

- [ ] **scene** 名 ①光景, 風景 ②(劇の)場, 一幕 ③(事件の)現場

- [ ] **scenic** 形 ①景色の, 景色のよい ②舞台の, 背景の

- [ ] **school** 名 学校, 校舎, 授業(時間)

- [ ] **science** 名 (自然)科学, 理科, ~学, 学問

- [ ] **scuba-diving** 名 スキューバダイビング

- [ ] **sea** 名 海,《the ~ S-, the S- of ~》~海

- [ ] **seamless** 形 〔移行などが〕途切れない, 滑らかな, 調和した

- [ ] **search** 動 捜し求める, 調べる 名 捜査, 探索, 調査 **in search of** ~を探し求めて

- [ ] **season** 名 ①季, 季節 ②盛り, 好機 動 味をつける

- [ ] **seasonal** 形 季節の

- [ ] **seat** 名 席, 座席, 位置 動 着席させる, すえつける

- [ ] **second** 名 ①第2(の人[物]) ②(時間の)秒, 瞬時 形 第2の, 2番の 副 第2に 動 後援する, 支持する

- [ ] **see** 動 ①見る, 見える, 見物する ②(~と)わかる, 認識する, 経験する ③会う ④考える, 確かめる, 調べる ⑤気をつける

- [ ] **seem** 動 (~に)見える, (~のように)思われる

- [ ] **seen** 動 see (見る)の過去分詞

- [ ] **Seimon-Ishibashi** 名 皇居正門石橋《皇居前広場から皇居に通じる石造の二連アーチ橋。一般的にこの橋が「二重橋」と思われているが, 正確にはこの奥に架かる「正門鉄橋」を指す》

- [ ] **selection** 名 選択(物), 選抜, 抜粋

- [ ] **sell** 動 売る, 売っている, 売れる

- [ ] **Sendagi** 名 千駄木《地名》

- [ ] **Sendai feudal domain** 仙台藩

- [ ] **sense** 名 ①感覚, 感じ ②《-s》意識, 正気, 本性 ③常識, 分別, センス ④意味 動 感じる, 気づく

- [ ] **Senso-ji Temple** 浅草寺《台東区浅草にある東京都内最古の寺。本尊は聖観世音菩薩》

- [ ] **sent** 動 send (送る)の過去, 過去分詞

- [ ] **separate** 動 ①分ける, 分かれる, 隔てる ②別れる, 別れさせる 形 分かれた, 別れた, 別々の

- [ ] **September** 名 9月

- [ ] **serene** 形 静かな, 穏やかな, うら

らかな

- **series** 名 一続き, 連続, シリーズ

- **serve** 動 ①仕える, 奉仕する ②(客の)応対をする, 給仕する, 食事[飲み物]を出す ③(役目を)果たす, 務める, 役に立つ

- **service** 名 ①勤務, 業務 ②公益事業 ③点検, 修理 ④奉仕, 貢献 動 保守点検する, (点検)修理をする

- **seven** 名 7(の数字), 7人[個] 形 7の, 7人[個]の

- **seventeenth** 名 17, 17人[個] 形 17の, 17人[個]の

- **several** 形 ①いくつかの ②めいめいの 代 いくつかのもの, 数人, 数個

- **shadow** 名 ①影, 暗がり ②亡霊 動 ①陰にする, 暗くする ②尾行する

- **shallow** 形 浅い, 浅はかな 名《the -s》浅瀬

- **shape** 名 ①形, 姿, 型 ②状態, 調子 動 形づくる, 具体化する

- **share** 名 ①分け前, 分担 ②株 動 分配する, 共有する

- **shaving** 名 ひげ[顔]を剃ること

- **Shiba Imperial Villa**《the former –》旧芝離宮恩賜庭園《港区にある都立庭園。江戸幕府の老中・大久保忠朝の上屋敷内に作庭した大名庭園楽寿園を起源とする》

- **Shibamata** 名 柴又《地名》

- **Shibuya** 名 渋谷《地名》

- **Shibuya Station** 渋谷駅《渋谷区道玄坂にある, JR東日本・京王電鉄・東急電鉄・東京メトロの駅》

- **Shinagawa** 名 品川《地名》

- **Shinagawa Station** 品川駅《港区にあるJR東日本・JR東海・JR貨物・京浜急行電鉄(京急)の駅》

- **Shinbashi** 名 新橋《地名》

- **shine** 動 ①光る, 輝く ②光らせる, 磨く 名 光, 輝き

- **Shinjuku** 名 新宿《地名》

- **Shinjuku Gyoen Park** 新宿御苑《新宿区と渋谷区にまたがる庭園。もとは江戸時代に信濃高遠藩内藤家の下屋敷があった敷地である》

- **Shinjuku Station** 新宿駅《新宿区・渋谷区にまたがって所在するJR東日本・京王電鉄・小田急電鉄・東京メトロ・都営地下鉄の駅。乗降客数が世界一多いことで有名》

- **Shinkansen** 名 新幹線

- **Shinobazu Pond** 不忍池《台東区・上野恩賜公園の中に位置する天然の池》

- **Shinobazu-dori Street** 不忍通り《東京都道437号のうち, 目白台2丁目～上野公園前交差点付近までの区間の通称》

- **Shin-Okubo (Station)** 名 新大久保《新宿区にあるJR東日本山手線の駅》

- **Shinto** 名 神道

- **Shiodome** 名 汐留《地名》

- **ship** 名 船, 飛行船 動 ①船に積む, 運送する ②乗船する

- **shitamachi** 名 下町《歴史的に, 江戸時代の御府内(江戸の市域)で低地にある町。対義語は, 高台の地域である「山の手」》

- **shochu** 名 焼酎

- **shogun** 名 将軍, 征夷大将軍

- **shogunate** 名〔日本の〕将軍の職[政治]

- **shop** 名 ①店, 小売り店 ②仕事場 動 買い物をする

- **shopper** 名 買い物客

- **shopping** 動 shop(買い物をする)の現在分詞 名 買い物

- **shore** 名 岸, 海岸, 陸

- **short** 形 ①短い ②背の低い ③不足している

- **shorten** 動〔～の長さを〕短くする, 短縮する

- **should** 助 ～すべきである, ～した

ほうがよい

- [ ] **show** 動①見せる, 示す, 見える ②明らかにする, 教える ③案内する 名①表示, 見世物, ショー ②外見, 様子
- [ ] **Showa** 名昭和時代《1926–1989》
- [ ] **Showa Emperor** 昭和天皇《日本の第124代天皇。1901–1989）》
- [ ] **shrine** 名廟, 聖堂, 神社
- [ ] **shut** 動①閉まる, 閉める, 閉じる ②たたむ ③閉じ込める ④shutの過去, 過去分詞
- [ ] **side** 名側, 横, そば, 斜面 **from one side to the other** 一方の側から他の側へ 形①側面の, 横の ②副次的な 動（〜の）側につく, 賛成する
- [ ] **sight** 名①見ること, 視力, 視界 ②光景, 眺め ③見解
- [ ] **sightseeing** 名観光, 見物
- [ ] **sign** 名①きざし, 徴候 ②跡 ③記号 ④身振り, 合図, 看板 動①署名する, サインする ②合図する
- [ ] **silence** 名沈黙, 無言, 静寂 動沈黙させる, 静める
- [ ] **silver** 名銀, 銀貨, 銀色 形銀製の
- [ ] **similar** 形同じような, 類似した, 相似の
- [ ] **similarly** 副同様に, 類似して, 同じように
- [ ] **since** 接①〜以来 ②〜だから 前〜以来 副それ以来
- [ ] **single-arched** 形単アーチの
- [ ] **site** 名位置, 敷地, 用地 動（ある場所に建物を）設ける, 位置させる
- [ ] **situated** 動situate（置く）の過去, 過去分詞 形位置した, （ある境遇に）ある
- [ ] **situation** 名①場所, 位置 ②状況, 境遇, 立場
- [ ] **sixteenth** 名第16番目（の人[物]）, 16日 形第16番目の
- [ ] **skewer** 名串, 焼き串 動串に刺す

- [ ] **sky** 名①空, 天空, 大空 ②天気, 空模様, 気候
- [ ] **skyscraper** 名超高層ビル, 摩天楼
- [ ] **slice** 名薄切りの1枚, 部分 動薄く切る
- [ ] **slightly** 副わずかに, いささか
- [ ] **slipper** 名スリッパ, 室内[舞踏]用の靴, 上履き, 室内履き
- [ ] **slope** 動傾斜する[させる], 坂になる, 勾配をつける 名坂, 斜面, 傾斜
- [ ] **small** 形①小さい, 少ない ②取るに足りない 副小さく, 細かく
- [ ] **smartphone** 名スマートフォン, スマホ
- [ ] **snack** 名軽食, おやつ 動軽食をとる
- [ ] **snow** 名雪 動雪が降る
- [ ] **snowy** 形雪の多い, 雪のように白い
- [ ] **so** 副①とても ②同様に, 〜もまた ③《先行する句・節の代用》そのように, そう **or so** 〜かそこらで **so many** 非常に多くの **so that** 〜するために, それで, 〜できるように **so 〜 that** … 非常に〜なので… 接①だから, それで ②では, さて
- [ ] **so-called** 形いわゆる, 〜といわれて
- [ ] **soba** 名そば《 = buckwheat noodle》
- [ ] **soba-ya** 名そば屋
- [ ] **Sobu Line** 総武線《千代田区の東京駅から千葉県銚子市の銚子駅を結ぶJR東日本の鉄道路線》
- [ ] **social** 形①社会の, 社会的な ②社交的な, 愛想のよい
- [ ] **society** 名社会, 世間
- [ ] **sold** 動sell（売る）の過去, 過去分詞
- [ ] **soldier** 名兵士, 兵卒
- [ ] **some** 形①いくつかの, 多少の ②ある, 誰か, 何か 副約, およそ 代①

いくつか ②ある人[物]たち

- □ **Somei-cho** 图染井町《現在の駒込にあたる旧地名》
- □ **Somei-Yoshino** 图ソメイヨシノ
- □ **somen** 图そうめん
- □ **sometimes** 副時々, 時たま
- □ **somewhat** 副いくらか, やや, 多少
- □ **sort** 图種類, 品質 **a sort of** ～のようなもの, 一種の～ 動分類する
- □ **sound** 图音, 騒音, 響き, サウンド
- □ **south** 图《the –》南, 南方, 南部 形南の, 南方[南部]の
- □ **southern** 形南の, 南向きの, 南からの
- □ **souvenir** 图〔旅行・出来事などの〕記念品,〔自分のための〕土産
- □ **space** 图①空間, 宇宙 ②すき間, 余地, 場所, 間 動間を空ける
- □ **spacious** 形広々とした, 広大な
- □ **speak** 動 speak (話す)の現在分詞 **Speaking of** ～について言えば 形話す, ものを言う 图話すこと, 談話, 演説
- □ **special** 形①特別の, 特殊の, 臨時の ②専門の
- □ **specialization** 图特殊化
- □ **specialize** 動専門にする, 専攻する, 特別にする
- □ **specific** 形明確な, はっきりした, 具体的な
- □ **speech** 图演説, 言語, 語
- □ **speed** 图速力, 速度
- □ **spent** 動 spend (使う)の過去, 過去分詞 形使い果たした, 疲れ切った
- □ **spiderweb** 图クモの巣
- □ **spirit** 图①霊 ②精神, 気力
- □ **split** 動裂く, 裂ける, 割る, 割れる, 分裂させる[する] 图①裂くこと, 割れること ②裂け目, 割れ目

- □ **sport** 图①スポーツ ②《-s》競技会, 運動会
- □ **sporting** 形スポーツの[に関する・用の]
- □ **spot** 图①地点, 場所, 立場 ②斑点, しみ 動①～を見つける ②点を打つ, しみをつける
- □ **sprang** 動 spring (跳ねる)の過去
- □ **spread** 動①広がる, 広げる, 伸びる, 伸ばす ②塗る, まく, 散布する **spread out** 広げる, 展開する 图広がり, 拡大
- □ **spring** 图①春 ②泉, 源 ③ばね, ぜんまい 動跳ねる, 跳ぶ **spring up** (急に)生じる, (ひょっこり)現れる
- □ **square** 图①正方形, 四角い広場, (市外の)一区画 ②2乗, 平方
- □ **stadium** 图スタジアム, 競技場
- □ **staff** 图職員, スタッフ 動配置する
- □ **stage** 图①舞台 ②段階 動上演する
- □ **stall** 图売店, 露店, 屋台
- □ **stand** 動①立つ, 立たせる, 立っている, ある ②耐える, 立ち向かう 图①台, 屋台, スタンド ②《the -s》観覧席 ③立つこと
- □ **stand-up** 形立って行う, 立ったままでする
- □ **standard** 图標準, 規格, 規準 形①標準の ②一流の, 優秀な
- □ **star** 图①星, 星形の物 ②人気者 形星形の
- □ **start** 動①出発する, 始まる, 始める ②生じる, 生じさせる **start doing** ～し始める 图出発, 開始
- □ **state** 图①あり様, 状態 ②国家, (アメリカなどの)州 ③階層, 地位 動述べる, 表明する
- □ **stately** 形堂々とした, 威厳のある
- □ **station** 图①駅 ②署, 局, 本部, 部署 動部署につかせる, 配置する
- □ **statue** 图像
- □ **status** 图①(社会的な)地位, 身分,

立場 ②状態

- □ **stay** 動①とどまる，泊まる，滞在する ②持続する，(〜の) ままでいる **stay in** (場所) に泊まる，滞在する 名滞在

- □ **steam** 名蒸気，湯気 動湯気を立てる

- □ **step** 名①歩み，1歩 (の距離) ②段階 ③踏み段，階段 動歩む，踏む **step back in time** 少し前の時代に戻る

- □ **stereotypical** 形型どおりの，ありふれた

- □ **stick** 名棒，杖 動①(突き) 刺さる，刺す ②くっつく，くっつける ③突き出る ④《受け身形で》いきづまる

- □ **still** 副①まだ，今でも ②それでも (なお) 形静止した，静かな

- □ **stone** 名①石，小石 ②宝石 形石の，石製の

- □ **stop** 動①やめる，やめさせる，止める，止まる ②立ち止まる 名①停止 ②停留所，駅

- □ **store** 名①店 ②蓄え ③貯蔵庫，倉庫 動蓄える，貯蔵する

- □ **storefront** 名①《米》〔道路に面した〕店の正面，店頭 ②《米》〔建物の道路に面した〕店舗

- □ **story** 名①物語，話 ②(建物の) 階

- □ **straw** 名麦わら，ストロー

- □ **street** 名①街路 ②《S-》〜通り

- □ **street-stall** 名露店

- □ **stress-free** 形ストレスのない

- □ **stretch** 動引き伸ばす，広がる，広げる **stretch out** 手足を伸ばす，背伸びする 名①伸ばす〔伸びる〕こと，広がり ②ストレッチ (運動)

- □ **strife** 名争い，不和

- □ **stroll** 名ぶらぶら歩き，散策 動ぶらぶら歩く，散歩する

- □ **stronghold** 名①〔戦いの〕要塞，とりで，牙城 ②〔活動などの〕拠点，本拠地

- □ **structure** 名構造，骨組み，仕組み 動組織立てる

- □ **study** 動①勉強する，研究する ②調べる 名①勉強，研究 ②書斎

- □ **stunning** 形①〈話〉気絶するほど〔驚くほど〕美しい，とても魅力的な ②見事な，素晴らしい ③びっくりする，驚くほどの

- □ **style** 名やり方，流儀，様式，スタイル

- □ **stylish** 形流行の，スタイリッシュな

- □ **subculture** 名〔社会の主流から外れた〕サブカルチャー，下位文化

- □ **suburb** 名近郊，郊外

- □ **subway** 名地下鉄，地下道

- □ **Subway Museum** 地下鉄博物館《江戸川区の東京メトロ東西線葛西駅の高架下にある，地下鉄を専門に扱った博物館》

- □ **successfully** 副首尾よく，うまく

- □ **such** 形①そのような，このような ②そんなに，とても，非常に **such ~ as** …〜のような〜 代そのような人〔物〕**such as** たとえば〜，〜のような

- □ **suffer** 動①(苦痛・損害などを) 受ける，こうむる ②(病気に) なる，苦しむ，悩む

- □ **Sugamo** 名巣鴨《地名》

- □ **Suica** 名スイカ《東日本旅客鉄道 (JR東日本) が発行し，JR東日本・東京モノレール・東京臨海高速鉄道などが発売するICカード乗車券》

- □ **Sumida** 名墨田《地名》

- □ **Sumida Hokusai Museum** すみだ北斎美術館《墨田区亀沢にある公立美術館。この界隈で生涯を送った江戸時代後期の浮世絵師・葛飾北斎の作品を展示している》

- □ **Sumida-gawa River** 隅田川《荒川から分岐し，東京湾に注ぐ全長23.5kmの河川》

- □ **summarize** 動要約する

□ **summer** 名夏

□ **sumo** 名相撲

□ **sunken** 形沈下した, 一段低い所にある(床・部屋など)

□ **sunny** 形①日当たりのよい, 日のさす ②陽気な, 快活な

□ **sunshine** 名日光

□ **supply** 動供給[配給]する, 補充する 名供給(品), 給与, 補充

□ **supporter** 名後援者, 支持者, サポーター, 支柱

□ **sure** 形確かな, 確実な,《be – to ~》必ず[きっと]~する, 確信して **make sure to** 必ず[確実に・忘れずに]~する 副確かに, まったく, 本当に

□ **surfing** 動surf(波に乗る)の現在分詞 名サーフィン

□ **surrender** 名降伏, 降参, 明け渡し 動降伏する, 引き渡す

□ **surround** 動囲む, 包囲する

□ **surrounding** 動surround(囲む)の現在分詞 名《-s》周囲の状況, 環境 形周囲の

□ **survival** 名生き残ること, 生存者, 残存物

□ **survive** 動①生き残る, 存続する, なんとかなる ②長生きする, 切り抜ける

□ **sushi** 名すし

□ **suspension bridge** つり橋

□ **sustain** 動持ちこたえる, 持続する, 維持する, 養う

□ **swampland** 名沼沢地

□ **swampy** 形沼地の(ような)

□ **sweet** 形①《-s》甘い菓子 ②甘い味[香り], 甘いもの

□ **swimming** 動swim(泳ぐ)の現在分詞 名水泳

□ **symbol** 名シンボル, 象徴

□ **system** 名制度, 系統, 体系, 秩序だった方法, 順序

T

□ **Tabata** 名田端《地名》

□ **table** 名①テーブル, 食卓, 台 ②一覧表 動卓上に置く, 棚上げにする

□ **tablet** 名①錠剤, タブレット ②便箋, メモ帳 ③銘板

□ **tactics** 名〔個々の〕戦術, 戦法

□ **Taisei Hokan** 《1867年11月9日, 江戸幕府第15代将軍・徳川慶喜が征夷大将軍の職を辞し, 政権を朝廷に返上することを申し出, 翌15日に天皇がそれを許可したこと》

□ **Taishakuten** 名柴又帝釈天, 帝釈天 題経寺(だいきょうじ)《葛飾区柴又にある日蓮宗の寺院の通称。正式名称は経栄山 題経寺(きょうえいざん だいきょうじ)》

□ **take** 動①取る, 持つ ②持って[連れて]いく, 捕らえる ③乗る ④(時間・労力を)費やす, 必要とする ⑤(ある動作を)する ⑥飲む ⑦耐える, 受け入れる **take care of** ~の世話をする, ~面倒を見る **take over** 引き継ぐ, 支配する, 乗っ取る **take place** 行われる, 起こる 名①取得 ②捕獲

□ **taken** 動take(取る)の過去分詞

□ **Takeshita-dori Street** 竹下通り《渋谷区神宮前または原宿にある商店通り・商店街》

□ **tale** 名①話, 物語 ②うわさ, 悪口

□ **talk** 動話す, 語る, 相談する 名①話, おしゃべり ②演説 ③《the –》話題

□ **tall** 形高い, 背の高い

□ **Tama Region** 多摩地域《東京都のうち, 東京23区と島嶼部(伊豆諸島・小笠原諸島)を除いた市町村部(26市・3町・1村)を指す》

□ **Tama-gawa River** 多摩川《山梨県・東京都・神奈川県を流れて東京湾に注ぐ河川》

□ **tap** 名①軽くたたくこと ②〔たるなどの〕口, 栓 ③〔たるから注いだ〕酒, ビール

□ **tapas** 名タパス《スペインの小皿料

159

理》

☐ **taste** 名①味, 風味 ②好み, 趣味 動味がする, 味わう

☐ **tatami** 名畳

☐ **taxi** 名タクシー 動①(飛行機が滑走路を)移動する ②タクシーで行く

☐ **Taxi Stand** 《米》タクシー乗り場

☐ **Tayasumon Gate** 田安門《千代田区北の丸公園内にある, 旧江戸城の門》

☐ **temperature** 名温度, 体温

☐ **temple** 名①寺, 神殿 ②こめかみ

☐ **tempura** 名天ぷら

☐ **ten** 名10(の数字), 10人[個] 形10の, 10人[個]の

☐ **terminal** 名①終着駅, ターミナル, 終点 ②端末

☐ **terrible** 形恐ろしい, ひどい, ものすごい, つらい

☐ **testing** 動test(試みる)の現在分詞 名テストすること

☐ **texture** 名①手触り, きめ ②織り方, 生地

☐ **than** 接~よりも, ~以上に **more than** ~以上 **than any other** ほかのどの~よりも

☐ **that** 形その, あの **at that time** その時 代①それ, あれ, その[あの]人[物] ②《関係代名詞》~である… 接~ということ, ~なので, ~だから **so that** ~するために, それで, ~できるように **so ~ that** … 非常に~なので… 副そんなに, それほど

☐ **the** 冠①その, あの ②《形容詞の前で》~な人々 副《 - + 比較級, - + 比較級》~すればするほど…

☐ **theater** 名劇場

☐ **theatrical** 形①劇の, 劇場の ②芝居じみた, わざとらしい

☐ **their** 代彼(女)らの, それらの

☐ **them** 代彼(女)らを[に], それらを[に]

☐ **then** 副その時(に・は), それから, 次に 名その時 形その当時の

☐ **there** 副①そこに[で・の], そこへ, あそこへ ②《 - is[are]~》~がある[いる] **get there** そこに到着する 名そこ

☐ **therefore** 副したがって, それゆえ, その結果

☐ **these** 代これら, これ 形これらの, この **these days** このごろ

☐ **they** 代①彼(女)らは[が], それらは[が] ②(一般の)人々は[が]

☐ **think** 動思う, 考える **think of ~** のことを考える, ~を思いつく, 考え出す

☐ **third** 名第3(の人[物]) 形第3の, 3番の

☐ **third-largest** 形〔規模が〕3番目に大きい, 第3位の

☐ **thirty-five** 名35(の数字) 形35の

☐ **this** 形①この, こちらの, これを ②今の, 現在の **at this time** 現時点では, このとき 代①これ, この人[物] ②今, ここ

☐ **those** 形それらの, あれらの 代それら[あれら]の人[物]

☐ **though** 接①~にもかかわらず, ~だが ②たとえ~でも **even though** ~であるけれども, ~にもかかわらず 副しかし

☐ **thousand** 名①1000(の数字), 1000人[個] ②《 - s》何千, 多数 **thousands of** 何千という 形①1000の, 1000人[個]の ②多数の

☐ **three** 名3(の数字), 3人[個] 形3の, 3人[個]の

☐ **through** 前~を通して, ~中を[に], ~中 副①通して ②終わりまで, まったく, すっかり **pass through** ~を通る, 通行する

☐ **throughout** 前①~中, - を通じて ②~のいたるところに 副初めから終わりまで, ずっと

☐ **ticket** 名切符, 乗車[入場]券, チケ

ット

□ **tidal** 形 潮の, 潮の干満による

□ **Tidal Basin** タイダルベイスン《ワシントン運河にポトマック川の水流を導き, その汚染を防止するために1897年に築かれた半人工的な入り江》

□ **time** 名 ①時, 時間, 歳月 ②時期 ③期間 ④時代 ⑤回, 倍 **any time** いつでも **at that time** その時 **at the time** そのころ, 当時は **at this time** 現時点では, このとき **on time** 時間どおりに **step back in time** 少し前の時代に戻る 動 時刻を決める, 時間を計る

□ **Times Square** 《米》タイムズ・スクエア《ニューヨークの7番街 (Seventh Avenue), 42番街 (42nd Street), ブロードウェイ (Broadway) が交差する広場》

□ **tiny** 形 ちっぽけな, とても小さい

□ **tip** 名 ①チップ, 心づけ ②先端, 頂点 動 ①チップをやる ②先端につける

□ **to** 前 ①《方向・変化》～へ, ～に, ～の方へ ②《程度・時間》～まで ③《適合・付加・所属》～に ④《＋動詞の原形》～するために [の], ～する, ～すること **from ～ to …** ～から…まで **up to** ～まで, ～に至るまで

□ **today** 名 今日 副 今日 (で) は

□ **together** 副 ①一緒に, ともに ②同時に

□ **toilet** 名 トイレ, 化粧室

□ **Tokaido** 名 東海道《江戸時代の江戸・日本橋を起点に伸びる五街道の一つで, 小田原・駿府・浜松・宮・桑名・草津を経て, 京都・三条大橋までの五十三次 (約490 km)》

□ **Tokaido Shinkansen** 東海道新幹線《東京駅から新大阪駅までを結ぶJR東海の高速鉄道路線 (新幹線)》

□ **Tokugawa Iemitsu** 徳川家光《江戸幕府の第3代将軍 (在職1623-1651)。1604-1651》

□ **Tokugawa Ieyasu** 徳川家康《江戸幕府を開いた初代将軍。織田信長・豊臣秀吉とともに「三英傑」の一人として知られる。1543-1616》

□ **Tokugawa Shogunate** 徳川幕府《徳川家康が征夷大将軍に任官し, 江戸を本拠として創設した武家政権。江戸幕府とも》

□ **Tokugawa-clan** 名 徳川氏《徳川家康が創始した日本の氏族》

□ **Tokyo** 名 東京《地名》

□ **Tokyo Bay** 東京湾

□ **Tokyo Disneyland** 東京ディズニーランド

□ **Tokyo DisneySea** 東京ディズニーシー

□ **Tokyo Dome** 東京ドーム《文京区後楽にあるドーム型野球場》

□ **Tokyo Midtown** 東京ミッドタウン《港区赤坂にある大規模複合施設》

□ **Tokyo Skytree** 東京スカイツリー《墨田区押上にある電波塔》

□ **Tokyo Station** 東京駅《千代田区丸の内にある, JR東日本・JR東海・東京メトロの駅》

□ **Tokyo Tower** 東京タワー《港区芝公園にある総合電波塔の愛称。正式名称は「日本電波塔」》

□ **Tokyoite** 名 東京都民, 都民, 東京人

□ **told** 動 tell (話す) の過去, 過去分詞

□ **too** 副 ①～も (また) ②あまりに～すぎる, とても～ **too ～ to …** …するには～すぎる

□ **took** 動 take (取る) の過去

□ **toothbrush** 名 歯ブラシ

□ **toothpaste** 名 練り歯磨き

□ **top** 名 頂上, 首位 **on top of** ～の上 (に) 形 いちばん上の

□ **topping** 名 トッピング, 上に乗せるもの

□ **torii** 名 鳥居

□ **total** 形 総計の, 全体の, 完全な 名 全体, 合計 動 合計する

□ **tough** 形 ①〔物が〕丈夫な, 頑丈な ②〔食べ物が〕固い

□ **tourist** 名 旅行者, 観光客

□ **toward** 前 ①《運動の方向・位置》〜の方へ, 〜に向かって ②《目的》〜のために

□ **tower** 名 塔, やぐら, 砦 動 ①そびえる ②抜き出る

□ **town** 名 町, 都会, 都市

□ **townspeople** 名 街の住人, 市民, 町民

□ **Toyosu Fish Market** 豊洲市場《江東区豊洲にある公設の卸売市場》

□ **Toyotomi Hideyoshi** 豊臣秀吉《関白・太政大臣に就任し, 天下統一を果たした武将。織田信長・徳川家康とともに「三英傑」の一人として知られる。1537-1598》

□ **trace** 名 ①跡 ②(事件などの)こん跡 動 たどる, さかのぼって調べる

□ **track** 名 ①通った跡 ②競走路, 軌道, トラック 動 追跡する

□ **trade** 名 取引, 貿易, 商業 動 取引する, 貿易する, 商売する

□ **traditional** 形 伝統的な

□ **traditionally** 副 伝統的に, 元々は

□ **train** 名 ①列車, 電車 ②(〜の)列, 連続 動 訓練する, 仕立てる

□ **tranquil** 形 静かな, 穏やかな

□ **transform** 動 〔〜の状態・形・外観・性質・機能などを〕変える, 転換[変換]する

□ **transformation** 名 変化, 変換, 変容

□ **transit** 名 通過, 乗り換え, トランジット

□ **transport** 動 〔物を〕運ぶ, 輸送する

□ **transportation** 名 交通(機関), 輸送手段

□ **travel** 動 ①旅行する ②進む, 移動する[させる], 伝わる 名 旅行, 運行

□ **traveler** 名 旅行者

□ **traverse** 動 〔場所を〕横切る, 横断する

□ **treasure** 名 財宝, 貴重品, 宝物 動 秘蔵する

□ **treat** 動 ①扱う ②治療する ③おごる

□ **tree** 名 ①木, 樹木, 木製のもの ②系図

□ **tree-lined** 形 並木の(ある)

□ **trellis** 名 ①格子, 格子型の紋 ②格子のアーチ[あずまや]

□ **trend** 名 ①傾向, 動向, トレンド ②流行, はやり

□ **trendsetting** 形 流行を作り出している[決めている]

□ **trillion** 名 1兆 形 1兆の

□ **trip** 名 (短い)旅行, 遠征, 遠足, 出張

□ **tropical** 形 熱帯の

□ **true** 形 ①本当の, 本物の, 真の ②誠実な, 確かな 副 本当に, 心から

□ **truly** 副 ①全く, 本当に, 真に ②心から, 誠実に

□ **try** 動 ①やってみる, 試みる ②努力する, 努める 名 試み, 試し

□ **Tsukiji Fish Market** 築地市場《中央区築地で1935〜2018年まで83年にわたって使用されていた公設の卸売市場》

□ **Tsukishima** 名 月島《地名》

□ **turn** 動 ①回転する, 向きを変える ②変化する, 〔変わって〜に〕なる **turn out** (結局〜に) なる

□ **TV** 名 〈話〉テレビ

□ **twentieth** 名 《the -》第20(の人・物) 形 《the -》第20の, 20番の

□ **twenty-four** 名 24 (の数字) 形 24の

□ **twenty-six** 名 26 (の数字) 形 26

の

□ **twenty-three** 图23（の数字）
形23の

□ **twice** 副2倍，2度，2回

□ **two** 图2（の数字），2人［個］ 形2の，
2人［個］の

□ **type** 图①型，タイプ，様式 ②見本，
模様，典型 動①典型となる ②タイ
プで打つ

□ **typhoon** 图台風，暴風

□ **typically** 副典型的に，いかにも～
らしく

U

□ **udon** 图うどん

□ **Ueno** 图上野《地名》

□ **Ueno Park** 上野恩賜公園《台東区
にある公園で通称「上野公園」。園内
には博物館，動物園等，多くの文化施
設が存在する》

□ **Ueno Station** 上野駅《台東区に
あるJR東日本・東京メトロの駅》

□ **Ueno Zoo** 恩賜上野動物園《台
東区の上野恩賜公園内にある東京都
立動物園。通称「上野動物園」》

□ **ukiyo-e** 图浮世絵

□ **unconditional** 形無条件の，絶
対的な

□ **under** 前①《位置》～の下［に］②
《状態》～で，～を受けて，～のもと
③《数量》～以下［未満］の，～より下
の 形下の，下部の 副下に［で］，従
属［服従］して

□ **underground** 形①地下の［にあ
る］②地下組織の ③前衛的な 图①
地下鉄，地下（道）②地下組織 ③前
衛運動

□ **underneath** 前～の下に，～真下
に 副下に［を］，根底は 图《the –》
底部

□ **understandable** 形理解できる，
わかる

□ **UNESCO** 略国際連合教育科学文
化機関，ユネスコ《= United Nations
Educational, Scientific and Cultural
Organization》

□ **unexpectedly** 副思いがけなく，
突然に

□ **unfortunately** 副不幸にも，運悪
く

□ **unhurried** 形急がない，ゆっくり
した，慎重な

□ **unification** 图統一，一体化

□ **unique** 形唯一の，ユニークな，独
自の

□ **uniquely** 副独自に，比類なく，一
意的に

□ **united** 動unite（1つにする）の過
去，過去分詞 形団結した，まとまった，
連合した

□ **university** 图（総合）大学

□ **unless** 接～でない限り，～である
場合を除いて，もし～でなければ

□ **unparalleled** 形並ぶ者のない，
ほかに例を見ない，前代未聞の

□ **until** 前～まで（ずっと）接～の時
まで，～するまで

□ **unusually** 形異常に，珍しく

□ **up** 副①上へ，上がって，北へ ②立
って，近づいて ③向上して，増して
grow up 成長する **open up to the
world** 世界に門戸を開く，対外開放
する **spring up**（急に）生じる，（ひ
ょっこり）現れる **up to** ～まで，～に
至るまで 前①～の上（の方）へ，高
い方へ ②（道）に沿って 形上向きの，
上りの 图上昇，向上，値上がり

□ **upgrading** 图①《性能などの》向
上，改善，増進 ②《等級などの》格上げ，
ランクアップ

□ **upscale** 形①《人が》上流階級の，
高所得（層）の ②《商品などが》高級
な ③《商売などが》金持ち相手の

□ **Urayasu** 图浦安《千葉県の地名》

□ **US-led** 形米国［アメリカ］主導の

- □ **use** 動 ①使う, 用いる ②費やす 名 使用, 用途
- □ **used** 動《use（使う）の過去, 過去分詞 ②《– to》よく～したものだ, 以前は～であった 形 ①慣れている, 《get［become］– to》～に慣れてくる ②使われた, 中古の
- □ **useful** 形 役に立つ, 有効な, 有益な
- □ **Ushigome Gate** 牛込門（牛込見附）《江戸城の外濠に設けられていた上州道に通じる北の関門》
- □ **usually** 副 普通, いつも（は）
- □ **utensil** 名〔主に台所の〕器具, 用具, 用品

V

- □ **vacation** 名（長期の）休暇
- □ **valley** 名 谷, 谷間
- □ **Van Gogh**《Vincent Willem –》ファン・ゴッホ《オランダのポスト印象派の画家。1853–1890》
- □ **variety** 名 ①変化, 多様性, 寄せ集め ②種類
- □ **various** 形 変化に富んだ, さまざまの, たくさんの
- □ **vegetable** 名 野菜, 青物 形 野菜の, 植物(性)の
- □ **vending machine**〔飲料などの〕自動販売機
- □ **Venice** 名 ヴェネチア, ヴェニス《イタリアの都市》
- □ **version** 名 ①バージョン, 版, 翻訳 ②意見, 説明, 解釈
- □ **very** 副 とても, 非常に, まったく 形 本当の, きわめて, まさしくその
- □ **vibrant** 形 響き渡る, 活気のある, (色が)鮮やかな
- □ **vicinity** 名 近所, 近辺, 付近
- □ **view** 名 ①眺め, 景色, 見晴らし ②考え方, 意見 動 眺める
- □ **villa** 名 邸宅, 別荘

- □ **village** 名 村, 村落
- □ **vinegared** 形 酢漬けの, 酢で味付けした
- □ **visit** 動 訪問する 名 訪問
- □ **visitor** 名 訪問者, 観光客, 滞在客
- □ **voice** 名 ①声, 音声 ②意見, 発言権 動 声に出す, 言い表す

W

- □ **waiting** 動《wait（待つ）の現在分詞 名 待機, 給仕すること 形 待っている, 仕えている
- □ **walk** 動 歩く, 歩かせる, 散歩する **walk along** (前へ)歩く, ～に沿って歩く **walk away** 立ち去る, 遠ざかる **walk to** ～まで歩いて行く 名 歩くこと, 散歩
- □ **walking** 動《walk（歩く）の現在分詞 名 歩行, 歩くこと 形 徒歩の, 歩行用の
- □ **wall** 名 ①壁, 塀 ②障壁 動 壁［塀］で囲む, ふさぐ
- □ **want** 動 ほしい, 望む, ～したい, ～してほしい 名 欠乏, 不足
- □ **war** 名 戦争(状態), 闘争, 不和 **civil war** 内戦, 内乱
- □ **ward** 名〔郡や市の行政〕区
- □ **warm** 形 ①暖かい, 温暖な ②思いやりのある, 愛情のある 動 暖まる, 暖める
- □ **warrior** 名 戦士, 軍人
- □ **warship** 名 軍艦
- □ **was** 動《be の第1・第3人称単数現在 am, is の過去》～であった, (～に)いた［あった］
- □ **Washington, D.C.** 名 ワシントン《米国の首都：州》
- □ **watch** 動 ①じっと見る, 見物する ②注意［用心］する, 監視する 名 ①警戒, 見張り ②腕時計
- □ **water** 名 ①水 ②(川・湖・海などの)

多量の水 動水を飲ませる, (植物に)水をやる

☐ **waterway** 名〔船が航行できる〕河川, 水路, 運河

☐ **wave** 名①波 ②(手などを) 振ること 動①揺れる, 揺らす, 波立つ ②(手などを振って)合図する

☐ **way** 名①道, 通り道 ②方向, 距離 ③方法, 手段 ④習慣 **on one's way home** 帰り道で **on one's way to ~** に行く途中で **on the way home** 帰宅途中に **way to ~** する方法

☐ **we** 代私たちは[が]

☐ **weakness** 名①弱さ, もろさ ②欠点, 弱点

☐ **wealthy** 形裕福な, 金持ちの

☐ **weather** 名天気, 天候, 空模様

☐ **web** 名〔複雑な構造の〕クモの巣状の[交錯した]物

☐ **week** 名週, 1週間

☐ **weekday** 名週日, 平日

☐ **well** 副①うまく, 上手に ②十分に, よく, かなり **as well** なお, その上, 同様に **as well as ~** と同様に 間へえ, まあ, ええと 形健康な, 適当な, 申し分ない 名井戸

☐ **well-earned** 形〔報酬・名声などが〕自分の力[懸命な働き]で勝ち得た

☐ **well-known** 形よく知られた, 有名な

☐ **were** 動《beの2人称単数・複数の過去》~であった, (~に)いた[あった]

☐ **west** 名《the -》西, 西部, 西方《the W-》西洋 形西の, 西方[西部]の, 西向きの 副西へ, 西方へ

☐ **western** 形①西の, 西側の ②《W-》西洋の 名《W-》西部劇, ウェスタン

☐ **Westerner** 名欧米人, 西洋人

☐ **wet-weather** 形雨天の, 多湿の

☐ **what** 代①何が[を・に] ②《関係代名詞》~するところのもの[こと] 形①何の, どんな ②なんと ③~するだけの 副いかに, どれほど

☐ **when** 副①いつ ②《関係副詞》~するところの, ~するとその時, ~するとき 接~の時, ~するとき 代いつ

☐ **where** 副①どこに[で] ②《関係副詞》~するところの, そしてそこで, ~するところ **where to** どこで~すべきか 接~なところに[へ], ~するところに[へ] 代①どこ, どの点 ②~するところの

☐ **whether** 接~かどうか, ~する間または…, ~であろうとなかろうと

☐ **which** 形①どちらの, どの, どれでも ②どんな~でも, そしてこの 代①どちら, どれ, どの人 [物] ②《関係代名詞》~するところの **of which** ~の中で

☐ **while** 接①~の間(に), ~する間(に) ②一方, ~なのに 名しばらくの間, 一定の時

☐ **who** 代①誰が[は], どの人 ②《関係代名詞》~するところの(人)

☐ **whole** 形全体の, すべての, 完全な, 満~, 丸~ 名《the -》全体, 全部 **as a whole** 全体として

☐ **wholesale** 名卸売り 形卸の, 大規模な

☐ **wholesaler** 名卸売販売業者, 問屋

☐ **whom** 代①誰を[に] ②《関係代名詞》~するところの人, そしてその人を

☐ **whose** 代①誰の ②《関係代名詞》(~の)…するところの

☐ **why** 副①なぜ, どうして ②《関係副詞》~するところの(理由) 間①おや, まあ ②もちろん, なんだって ③ええと

☐ **wide** 形幅の広い, 広範囲の, 幅が~ある 副広く, 大きく開いて

☐ **widely** 副広く, 広範囲にわたって

A
B
C
D
E
F
G
H
I
J
K
L
M
N
O
P
Q
R
S
T
U
V
W
X
Y
Z

□ **will** 助 ～だろう, ～しよう, する (つもりだ) 名決意, 意図

□ **winding** 形 曲がりくねった, 回りくどい

□ **window** 名 窓, 窓ガラス

□ **winter** 名 冬 動 冬を過ごす

□ **wipe** 動 ～をふく, ぬぐう, ふきとる 名 ふくこと

□ **wisteria trellis** 藤棚

□ **with** 前 ①《同伴・付随・所属》～と一緒に, ～を身につけて, ～とともに ②《様態》～(の状態) で, ～して ③《手段・道具》～で, ～を使って

□ **within** 前 ①～の中 [内] に, ～の内部に ②～以内で, ～を越えないで 副中 [内] へ [に], 内部に 名内部

□ **without** 前 ～なしで, ～がなく, ～しないで **it goes without saying** ～は言うまでもない, ～に決まっている

□ **women** 名 woman (女性) の複数

□ **won** 動 win (勝つ) の過去, 過去分詞

□ **wonderful** 形 驚くべき, すばらしい, すてきな

□ **wonderland** 名 おとぎの国, 不思議の国, すばらしい場所 [土地]

□ **wood** 名 ①《しばしば-s》森, 林 ②木材, まき

□ **woodblock** 名 木版 (画)

□ **wooded** 形 森のある, 森林の多い

□ **wooden** 形 木製の, 木でできた

□ **word** 名 ①語, 単語 ②ひと言 ③《one's ～》約束

□ **work** 動 ①働く, 勉強する, 取り組む ②機能 [作用] する, うまくいく 名 ①仕事, 勉強 ②職 ③作品 **works of art** 芸術作品

□ **worker** 名 仕事をする人, 労働者

□ **working** 動 work (働く) の現在分詞 形 働く, 作業の, 実用的な

□ **world** 名《the ～》世界, ～界 **all over the world** 世界中に **in the world** 世界で **open up to the world** 世界に門戸を開く, 対外開放する

□ **World Heritage** 世界遺産

□ **World War Two** 第二次世界大戦《1939-1945》

□ **world-famous** 形 世界的に有名な

□ **worth** 形 (～の) 価値がある, (～) しがいがある 名 価値, 値打ち

□ **would** 助《willの過去》①～するだろう, ～するつもりだ ②～したものだ

□ **wrestling** 動 wrestle (取っ組み合う) の現在分詞 名 レスリング

□ **wrong** 形 ①間違った, (道徳上) 悪い ②調子が悪い, 故障した 副 間違って 名 不正, 悪事

Y

□ **Yaesu Entrance** 八重洲口《東京駅の東側にある出口。八重洲北口・八重洲中央口・八重洲南口・八重洲地下中央口がある》

□ **yagiri no watashi** 矢切の渡し《江戸時代に設けられた江戸川の農民渡し舟で, 葛飾区柴又と千葉県松戸市の矢切を結んでいる》

□ **yakitori** 名 焼き鳥

□ **yakitori-ya** 名 焼き鳥屋

□ **Yamanashi Prefecture** 山梨県

□ **yamanote** 名 山の手《歴史的に, 江戸時代の御府内 (江戸の市域) で高台の地域。対義語は, 低地にある町を指す「下町」》

□ **Yamanote Line** 山手線《JR東日本が運営する鉄道路線。港区の品川駅を起点に, 渋谷駅, 新宿駅, 池袋駅を経由して北区の田端駅とを結ぶ》

□ **Yanaka** 名 谷中《地名》

□ **Yanaka Ginza** 谷中銀座《台東区谷中にある商店街》

166

□ **Yanaka Reien** 谷中霊園《台東区
谷中にある都立霊園。徳川15代将軍・
慶喜や鳩山一郎・横山大観・渋沢栄一
などが眠る》

□ **Yanesen** 谷根千《文京区東端から
台東区西端一帯の谷中、根津、千駄木
周辺地区を指す総称。それぞれの地名
の頭文字から》

□ **Yasukuni-dori Street** 靖国通
り《新宿区・千代田区・中央区を東西
に走る東京都道302号新宿両国線の
通称》

□ **Yasukuni-jinja** 名 靖国神社《千
代田区九段北にある神社。国家のため
に殉難した軍人・軍属等の霊（英霊）
を祀る》

□ **yatai** 名 屋台

□ **year** 名 ①年、1年 ②学年、年度 ③
〜歳 **for** 〜 **years** 〜年間、〜年にわ
たって

□ **Yebisu Beer** エビスビール《サッ
ポロビールが製造・販売する麦芽100
％ビールの商標》

□ **yokocho** 名 横丁

□ **Yokohama** 名 横浜《神奈川県の地
名》

□ **Yotsuya** 名 四谷《地名》

□ **you** 代 ①あなた（方）は［が］、あな
た（方）を［に］②（一般に）人は

□ **young** 形 若い、幼い、青年の

□ **your** 代 あなた（方）の

□ **yourself** 代 あなた自身

□ **youth** 名 若さ、元気、若者

□ **Yurakucho** 名 有楽町《地名》

□ **Yurikamome Line** ゆりかもめ
《港区の新橋駅から江東区の豊洲駅ま
でを結ぶ路線の愛称。正式名称は「東
京臨海新交通臨海線」》

□ **Yushima-Seido** 名 湯島聖堂《文
京区湯島にある史跡。江戸幕府5代将
軍・徳川綱吉によって建てられた孔
子廟であり、後に幕府直轄の学問所と
なった》

Z

□ **zero** 名 ゼロ、零、どん底、最低点
形 ゼロ［零］の

□ **Zojo-ji Temple** 増上寺《港区芝公
園にある、浄土宗の七大本山の一つ。
徳川家の菩提寺で、2代・秀忠、6代・
家宣、7代・家継、9代・家重、12代・家慶、
14代・家茂の墓所が設けられている》

English Conversational Ability Test
国際英語会話能力検定

● E-CATとは…
英語が話せるようになるための
テストです。インターネット
ベースで、30分であなたの発
音力をチェックします。

www.ecatexam.com

● iTEP®とは…
世界各国の企業、政府機関、アメリカの大学
300校以上が、英語能力判定テストとして採用。
オンラインによる90分のテストで文法、リー
ディング、リスニング、ライティング、スピー
キングの5技能をスコア化。iTEP®は、留学、就
職、海外赴任などに必要な、世界に通用する英
語力を総合的に評価する画期的なテストです。

www.itepexamjapan.com

ラダーシリーズ
Exploring Tokyo 英語で読む東京

2020年9月4日 第1刷発行

著　者　西海コエン

発行者　浦　晋亮

発行所　**IBCパブリッシング株式会社**
　　　　〒162-0804 東京都新宿区中里町29番3号
　　　　菱秀神楽坂ビル9F
　　　　Tel. 03-3513-4511　Fax. 03-3513-4512
　　　　www.ibcpub.co.jp

© IBC Publishing, Inc. 2020

印刷　中央精版印刷株式会社
装丁　伊藤 理恵

Printed in Japan
ISBN978-4-7946-0637-2